DEVELOPING YOURSELF,
YOUR CAREER AND
YOUR ORGANIZATION

The Mike Pedler Library
Developing people and organizations
General Editor: Dr Mike Pedler
Published by Lemos & Crane, London

Also available in this series:

Reg Revans
ABC of Action Learning

Nancy M. Dixon
Dialogue at Work

Mike Pedler and Kath Aspinwall
A Concise Guide to the Learning Organization

Mike Pedler and Tom Boydell
Managing Yourself

Rennie Fritchie and Malcolm Leary
Resolving Conflicts in Organizations

"The books are easy to read, well set out and full of useful prompts and activities that will aid managers in explaining key issues.".
Chris Bones, HR Director Europe, UDV

For more information visit us at **www.lemosandcrane.co.uk**

Developing Yourself, Your Career and Your Organization

JOHN BURGOYNE

Lemos&Crane

This edition first published in Great Britain 1999
Lemos & Crane
20 Pond Square
Highgate Village
London N6 6BA
http://www.lemosandcrane.co.uk

ISBN 1-898001-40-5

A CIP catalogue record for this book is available from the British Library.

Designed and typeset by DAP Ltd, London
Printed and bound by Redwood Books, Trowbridge

Contents

Introduction to the Library

"All learning is for the sake of action, and all action for the sake of friendship." John Macmurray

The supposed end of certainty, and with it the arts of prediction and strategic planning, has led some managers to contemplate notions of paradox, chaos and boundlessness, multiple dilemmas and complexity theory. Others, struggling with the intractable problems of organization, have turned to re-engineering and quality management, only to find that these apparently novel solutions turn out to be old wine in new bottles, the descendants of Taylorism and Fordism.

To be responsive to change, a child, adult, organization, even a society, must be adept at learning. Learning is the means of acquiring new knowledge and skill, but also of making sense of our lives – individually and collectively – in increasingly fragmented times. In the absence of a reliable plan or blueprint for success, we can go on hopefully to learn our way forwards, recognizing what we cannot do, yet growing in confidence, making our own path.

For individuals, a fourth 'R' – Responsive to Change – must now be added to the traditional school curriculum of Reading, Writing and Arithmetic. The individual learner is at the heart of organizations and societies grappling with unprecedented change and its consequences. Only those able to create some measure of order in themselves can create order and purpose in those around them. In the absence of predictable employment, careers and lives, we must become adept at learning new ways, new identities.

For organizations, with an average lifespan of forty years and declining, learning has become essential for survival (De Geus). Organizational learning as also been suggested as the only sustainable source of competitive advantage (Senge) and the single most important quality that can be developed and traded (Garratt).

In communities and society new efforts at partnership, collaborative action and learning in public forums to tackle the 'wicked' problems of poverty, inequality, pollution, crime and public safety are replacing the old choices of left or right, public or private, electoral democracy or entrepreneurial leadership.

When we discard old mind-sets, search for new directions, learning is at a premium. At all levels the questions are the same: how can we develop what we do best in order to trade and learn *and* avoid the undesirable downsides? How can we release individual energy, potential, self-reliance, active citizenship *and* build wealth, well-being, collective security and the quality of all our lives?

★

If individuals who are able to manage and develop themselves are the cornerstones of this new society, it is equally plain that in an era characterized by large organizations, that learning must extend to wider relationships in teams, companies, and increasingly, between organizations themselves. The new optimism of the 'learning organization' has emerged as part of this understanding, but even this does not go far enough. There are problems aplenty to defeat even the very best of our organizations standing alone; there is a need to organize action and learning in coalitions and partnerships of agencies to respond to these pressing tasks.

The need is scarcely yet glimpsed, let alone grasped, but in an ideal collaboration such as a 'learning society', there is: a freedom to learn – and not to learn – for individuals; an organizational desire to support the learning of all members and stakeholders *and* a vision to transform the organization as a whole in creating new products, services and relationships; together with equal opportunities in learning for all citizens, not least so that they might contribute to communities and societies that are good places in which to live. This manifesto is of course a re-interpretation of old revolutionary aspirations: *Liberty* for individuals, the ruling value of *Fraternity* for organizations, and a duty of *Equality* of treatment and opportunity in the social sphere. To each of these we hope to make a contribution, with ideas ranging from personal self-development, through organizational learning to transformations in communities and social policies.

★

The books in the Library are concerned with learning and action on the pressing issues facing us as people living and working in organizations, cities and societies. And whilst there is no single philosophy here, there is an implied criticism of the economic and cultural consensus which underlies much of the business and management literature in particular. There are challenges here for those who tend to assume that our future rests on the 'roll out' of global, information-based capitalism supported by the spread of liberal democracy. There is support for those who question whether the individual and organizational development aimed at 'high performance' or 'excellence' always leads to desirable outcomes. The irony of the self-proclaimed 'learning organization' which is still not a healthy place for people to work in or to live next to, is also noted.

Action and learning require more than just good ideas. In terms of content, each book in the Library contains:

- *educational input:* ideas of substance that you need to know about

- *invitations to action:* suggestions in the texts when you stop reading and go to do something with the ideas in order to learn

- *ethical and political elements:* moral support in action and learning about being an honest colleague, seeking good purposes or doing the right thing in difficult circumstances for those operating in dilemma-laden territory.

Though they aim to be attractive and accessible these books are not 'easy reads'. They offer the reader an invitation to self-confrontation. Suspicious of easy answers and not content with theory, they offer a middle ground of active methods and approaches to the problems and questions posed. Even on questions to which there are no obvious solutions, there are directions to follow to engage your personal energies, the support of colleagues and the aspirations of clients and customers. I hope you can't put one of these books down without at least thinking of doing something differently.

MIKE PEDLER

Introduction

If you are or hope to be a manager, and wish to develop yourself, your career and the organizations you work for, this book is for you. Looked at creatively, any organization you work in offers you:

- a major resource for self-development;

- a challenging environment where you can create and follow the career you want;

- an opportunity to contribute and add to its success, and through this make a contribution to society.

Most organizations have systems and opportunities:

- for education, training and development;

- for career and performance management;

- to be briefed on, comment on and even contribute to forming local and general policy.

All organizations have informal processes that do the same things.

If you understand the formal and informal processes of self, career and organizational development you will be able to:

- make maximum use of formal and informal learning opportunities;

- increase your employability;

- follow the career you want;

- help your organization do the same thing - develop, choose and achieve its strategic direction to become a learning organization in which you are a crucial member.

This book is also intended for specialists involved in the provision of learning opportunities, and career and organizational development. It provides an overall framework where these activities are integrated with each other and the business of the organization. For such professionals and specialists this book should help their 'clients' become better partners in the development process - it is like a simple book on health that helps people have more intelligent and useful conversations with their doctors.

*

The book has eight Chapters and a Workbook of 14 Activities to help you apply the ideas to yourself and your work situation. The Activities are collected together at the end of the book and a 'button arrow' in the text marks each Activity and where it can be found.

Chapter 1 states the main argument of the book: that you manage your career and development in partnership with the organizations you work with or for during your working life; and that you do this through a better understanding of how organizations work.

Chapter 2 offers you a way of understanding how organizations do or should work in evolving and implementing their strategies - forming and reforming people's careers as they do so and of how people learn and develop to perform to their own and to other people's satisfaction as this process unfolds.

Chapter 3 sets out the most important issues in the formal and informal processes by which people move between jobs to create emerging careers.

Chapter 4 describes the main formal and informal learning and development opportunities and methods, and offers ways of thinking about how they work, and how you can use them actively.

Chapter 5 deals with how personal development and career forming can be linked, both from your own and the organization's point of view. It uses one main example as an illustration of how this can be shaped from both sides.

Chapter 6 shows how all of the above is influenced by the different forms that organizational culture can take. It shows how this comes to the surface and has effect through the 'psychological contract', defined as the patterns of mutual expectations and obligations that evolve between you and the organizations and people you work with.

Chapter 7 clarifies some contemporary jargon to empower you in discussions about your career and development. As well as describing and explaining the key terms, the chapter outlines some of the issues, strengths and weaknesses associated with the practices they represent.

Chapter 8 shows how all these ideas and suggestions for managing your development and career can be part of a wider process of creating learning organizations or companies - where their overall development and your own can be linked together to mutual advantage.

1 Managing Your Career and Your Personal Development

If you want to have a successful, fulfilling and productive career in management where you grow and develop, feel you do worthwhile work and improve the quality of the organization you work in, you need to understand your organization's formal and informal management development processes.

KEY IDEAS

Managing is different from other activities. This is because it deals primarily with uncertainty in organizations - this has important implications for what you need to learn and how you develop your career. Managing is dealing with all the messy problems that are left when you remove those that can be dealt with by routine solutions, specialist technical and professional work. This messiness is what makes managing a special case from the point of view of learning and of developing a career.

Your career is the biography of your working life - often summarized as a sequence of roles, and is created by a series of deals and negotiations that you conduct with organizations and employers. Your career is negotiated by you. Organizational management development includes organizational practices and procedures that are on the other end of the negotiating process. If you understand these better, you can deal with them better.

Your career has two aspects: the structural and the developmental. The structure of your career is the things you have done, and the order in which you achieved them. The developmental aspect of your career is about how you change, learn and develop the knowledge, abilities and values that you acquire through both formal and informal learning.

The structural and developmental aspects of your career interact. What you learn affects the jobs and roles that are available to you in the future. Your jobs and roles affect what you can learn. Some people enter career and development cul-de-sacs where they develop highly specialist skills in work that becomes increasingly obsolete. They then find themselves with a very low level of employability. Others develop skills and accumulate experiences that are increasingly in demand and have their career options broadened as a consequence. Either can happen through luck or chance, but with a little awareness of the processes they can be managed.

Organizational management development impacts on you in one of two ways - either through 'structural tactics' - processes that structure your career - or 'developmental tactics' - learning opportunities that are offered to or imposed on you. If your organization is well set up developmentally there will be a coherent strategy behind the tactics that impact on you. Such a strategy should have the following benefits:

- Developmental and structural tactics will be aligned: development will support you in your current work and/or in preparing for future career options; future career possibilities and plans will be supported by appropriate learning opportunities; and these connections will be transparent and agreed between you and your organization.

- Career and job moves will be planned in discussion with colleagues and human resource specialists, where you will share understandings of:

  1. What jobs and activities are staying the same in your organization;

  2. What known changes are being phased in, and the challenges, threats, and opportunities that this creates for you;

3. How you may be able to shape future activity presently considered uncertain or unplanned.

- You should not find yourself preparing for a job that is going to disappear in next year's re-organization. You should feel that you participate in the discussion of what the organizational future will and should be like, and that decisions made take into account, and take advantage of, the cumulative managerial talent of which you are part.

Organizations vary on how well they deliver effective corporate management development. It is useful to think of seven levels of effectiveness as sketched in Figure 1 on page 8; these will be explored in more detail later.

The theoretical rationale for these levels, and some evidence that higher levels lead to greater organizational efficiency, will be presented later in this chapter.

How does this fit with your experience? Activity 1 on p.104 is the first of a series of exercises in this book that helps your evaluation.

ACTIVITY 1 Page 104

Most management development professionals agree that the model in Figure 1 is a correct description of what should be done and what they aspire to. Many would frankly admit that their organization is only at the middle rather than the higher levels of efficiency at the moment, and surveys and research suggest that this is generally true. Do not be surprised, or unduly despondent, therefore, if you conclude that you work for a 'middle range' or even 'low range' organization. In fact, if this is the case, it provides an opportunity. When you better understand the model, you

Fig.1
Effective Corporate Management Development Policy:
Initial Sketch of the Seven Levels

Level 6
As Level 5 and new policies are implemented as learning experiments, and I feel part of this.

Level 5
As Level 4 and I can see how my skills and visions, and those of my colleagues, influence the policies we are implementing.

Level 4
I pursue learning opportunities to support career plans for myself that fit in with what is know and planned about the future of the organization.

Level 3
I have learning opportunities and career discussions that do fit together and influence each other, but it is not clear how they relate to changes in where the organization is going.

Level 2
Specific, isolated events to do with learning or career development occasionally impact on me, but are disconnected from anything else.

Level 1
Everything to do with learning and career development is left to chance, but the informal processes allow me to have some influence on my future, and to prepare myself for it.

Level 0
I am unable to form any view of the future of my work, or to prepare for the future, through either formal or informal processes.

should be able to make the organization 'behave' at a higher level for you. This will be to the advantage of yourself, your organization and your colleagues.

If you are reasonably assertive, without being unrealistic, in the way you interact with formal and informal management development systems in your organization, you can make them work at higher levels of efficiency for you and the local part of the organization in which you work. This should be welcomed and encouraged by the management development specialists who will appreciate grass roots support in improving the efficiency of their own work.

The rest of this chapter elaborates the above and concentrates in particular on explaining what an efficient management development system in an organization looks like, and why and how it works. It offers a way of assessing your organization, and discusses how you should manage and negotiate your own learning and career development in the light of this assessment.

WHAT IS SPECIAL ABOUT MANAGEMENT?

As suggested earlier, managing is different from other activities at work in that it deals primarily with uncertainty in organizations. This has important implications for what you need to learn and how you develop your career. A good description of managing is • dealing with all the messy problems which are left when you take out those that can be dealt with by routine solutions, specialist and professional work. This messiness is what makes managing different and a special case from the point of view of learning it and developing a career in it. Further, it is universal to organizational life (though it may or may not be labelled as such), and has some special features that make it necessary to treat it differently.

Definitions and descriptions of management vary considerably. You may or may not have the word 'manager' in your job title, but if you are arranging things in general you are a manager. Classical definitions of managing differentiate planning, organizing, staffing, monitoring and controlling. Some definitions and descriptions deal with the rational, material side: allocating scarce resources; or setting up and running work systems on rational efficiency principles. This is often called scientific management.

Other descriptions emphasize the human aspect and describe managing as 'getting things done with and through people', often characterized as the 'human relations approach'. All these definitions contain some truth. However, the main distinguishing feature from a personal, career and organizational development perspective is management's concern with tackling uncertainty on behalf of organizations. This is what distinguishes it from other relatively routine operational, technical and professional work that organizations rely on to function, and for which people also need to be trained and developed.

The questions in Activity 2 on p.106 help you consider whether you are a manager.

Herb Simon and Reg Revans, two of the founding thinkers of management and management development, best express this perspective. Simon suggests that all activities in organizations can be divided into two categories: 'programmed', for which there is a formula or answer; and 'unprogrammed', those for which there is no formula or no answer. The latter have to be dealt with by innovation. Revans makes the similar if not identical distinction between human performance that comes from 'P' - learnt solutions to standard problems that can be repeated - and 'Q' - dilemmas for which there is no preformed solution. 'P' can be thought of as procedures that can be learnt as off-the-shelf solutions to regularly occurring and well understood problems. 'Q' can be thought of the quest and questioning that is necessary to find an approach to a unique and non-standard problem.

The learning and development that prepares people for un-programmed work and 'Q' activities is very different from preparing people to apply 'P' solutions to routine problems. For the latter, specific training with clear and specific objectives is possible and systematic training is an appropriate approach. In terms of careers, very specific job descriptions are possible. 'Q' activities and dealing with unprogrammed problems call for different human abilities: creativity, judgment, intelligence, insight. These are general, less specific, abilities that are developed rather than trained.

Defining managing as that part of organizational work that deals primarily with the unprogrammed, or 'Q', is useful for development purposes. This is because learning to deal with programmed problems or 'P' aspects of performance, involves actions that are known in advance to work, and which are fairly clearly understood. This cannot apply to the unprogrammed, or 'Q'. Theoretically and in practice developing managers is a fundamentally different kind of challenge - as is planning your job and career - precisely because this work cannot be defined in detail in advance.

YOUR CAREER AS THE PRODUCT OF A SERIES OF 'DEALS' YOU STRIKE WITH ORGANIZATIONS

Your career is the biography of your working life, often summarized as a sequence of roles, and is created by a series of deals and negotiations that you conduct with organizations and employers.

The negotiated nature of careers may be apparent from your own experience.

You will be employed in an organization as a result of a job offer by an employer, and an acceptance by you. Prior to that there will have been a two-way exchange on terms and conditions, work and responsibilities, effort and reward. Prior to that there will have been processes of application and recruitment, short listing, selection, and so on. Job changes internal to organizations will have similar but not identical dynamics. Of course, power is rarely equal in the negotiation - sometimes the individual has a rare skill and is in a 'seller's market'. Often the organization may find several people with suitable skills, and be in a position to pick and choose. However it is still a negotiation and assessing the power balance is part of the process.

In his classic book on this subject Ed Schein develops the idea of the negotiated nature of careers, and suggests two stages to the negotiation process: information exchange and deal making. He argues that the quality of deal making is often poor, with costly consequences for employer and employee, because the prior information-exchange stage is skimped, skipped or dealt with too briefly. Demanding more detailed information, and scrutinizing the information that is taken into account about you when decisions on the structure of your career and your development are made, will improve the quality of these negotiations.

Now consider your own career to date. Activity 3 on p.108 enables you to chronicle your career so far.

After completing Activity 3, continue on to Activity 4 on p.109. This enables you to establish how you found yourself at each career stage.

THE TWO FACES OF YOUR CAREER: DEVELOPMENT AND STRUCTURE

Corporate management development affects you most directly through its tactics, since you are its target, subject or client. These tactics tend to fall into the two categories: structural and developmental. Examples of structural tactics are annual appraisal, succession planning and assessment centres - these are discussed in Chapter 2. Developmental activities - courses, programmes, and so on - are intended to help you improve your current and future job performance and are the subject of Chapter 3. There are also hybrid activities, such as developmental assessment centres, intended to give you feedback as part of your personal development but also providing the organization with a measure of your potential for other job opportunities. These are dealt with in Chapter 4. Chapters 2, 3 and 4 are intended firstly to help you understand these activities, and secondly to help you make best use of them.

Activity 5 on p.110 will help you reflect on the 'structural' and 'developmental' tactics that you are aware of in your organization, and which you have experienced.

How these two aspects of a career - structural and developmental - can be analyzed for an individual is shown in Figure 2 on p.14.

Fig.2: An example of the interaction of learning and career steps: Mr/Ms X

Significant Career Steps	What did you do?	What did you study?	What did you learn in this period?	How have you used this – at the time or later?
Design Engineer	Technical design work.	Completed professional qualifications.	That there is intuition in design work; and to work with others.	Yes – all the time.
Project leader	Managed projects on design.	Nothing formal.	That you have to deal with people as individuals.	Yes – especially in operational projects.
Technical marketing adviser	Investigated clients technical requirements.	Nothing formal.	A marketing orientation and the cost/quality trade off.	As part of a broader awareness of how business works.
Production planner	Overall planning of production work including monitoring.	Short course on project management.	Techniques of scheduling, the need to talk to people all the time and how to influence without formal power.	Still doing it.

Now consider how these facets apply to your career. Activity 6 on p. 113 invites you to do a similar analysis for yourself to the one in Figure 2.

How MANAGEMENT DEVELOPMENT IMPLEMENTS AND IMPROVES CORPORATE STRATEGY

For the right managers with the right abilities to be in the right jobs in the right structure over time, to allow strategy to be implemented and improved, and for people to have rewarding careers corporate management development policy needs to integrate three components: corporate strategy, developmental tactics and structural tactics of career development. Figure 3 on p.16 illustrates how these elements relate to the seven levels shown in Figure 2.

As a manager you are likely to be on the receiving end of career management structural tactics - processes your organization uses to negotiate career changes (see Chapter 2 for full discussion), and learning and developmental tactics - courses and programmes intended to help you learn (see Chapter 3 for full discussion).

If these tactics are to do more than solve local and short-term problems, and contribute to the development of yourself, your career and the organization as a whole, there needs to be an underlying working strategy. Such a strategy should have a direct impact on you.

In the first instance, the strategy should recognize that much learning takes place naturally as a result of people taking an intelligent, experimental and inquisitive interest in their work experience, as does much of the background information sharing that informs career offers and choices taken more formally. More

Fig.3
Effective Corporate Management Development Policy

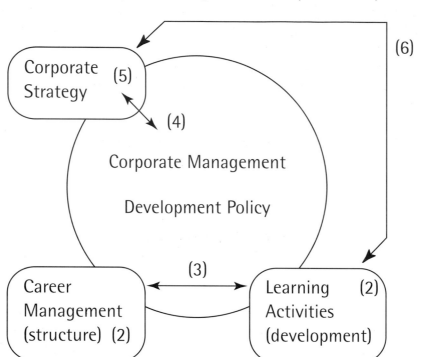

(1 - reliance on natural, informal processes)
(0 - natural, informal processes broken down)

deliberate and systematic management development activities need to acknowledge, build on and support these natural processes.

In some early research (J.G. Burgoyne and R. Stuart (1976) 'The nature, use and acquisition of managerial skills and other attributes' *Personal Review* 5(4) pp.19-29) my co-author and I estimated that about 80 per cent of the abilities that managers use in doing their work came from 'natural' sources - on the job trial and error, copying others (or avoiding their mistakes) and picking up ideas and trying them out. This contrasts with the 20 per cent from 'contrived' learning - learning from courses or any event defined as deliberately set up for useful learning. We arrived at this estimate by asking a sample of managers (a) to describe an activity or project where they believed they had performed effectively, then (b) to work out what skills and abilities they had used to allow them to do this, then (c) to decide how they acquired those skills and abilities. Then we analysed with them whether the source of the learning was primarily 'natural' or 'contrived'.

Try this out for yourself. At this point try Activity 7 on p.114 to explore your 'natural' learning experiences.

Secondly, the underlying strategy needs to ensure that the structural and the developmental are linked. If an annual appraisal or assessment of career potential leads to the designation of learning needs operating systems should follow this up by aligning you with available development opportunities. Equally, it should be clear how any learning events in which you participate fit with what you are intended and are intending to learn about, and how they support short and long-term career plans and possibilities.

To help you see the link between structural and developmental tactics, complete Activity 8 on p.115.

Thirdly, discussions, planning and exploration of possible future career scenarios should be informed by knowledge and judgment about the future activities, structures and job opportunities within the organization. A discussion about your future career that suggests a journey across the current organizational chart, should ring alarm bells as the chart is only likely to be a valid map in the short term.

For example, the elaborate career planning system of a division of a major chemical company, which had supported training at all pre-defined career stages, was rendered obsolete overnight when a sudden restructuring did away with most of the jobs for which the scheme had carefully planned and prepared people.

Equally, developmental activities that are intended to prepare you for the medium or long-term future should be based on some attempt to envisage the abilities that will be needed in the future, rather than on cloning manager profiles seen to be successful in the past. As the future is uncertain beyond a certain time horizon for all organizations, allowances should be made. This can be achieved through developing career plans with multiple scenarios, contingencies, and general abilities that are applicable across a range of situations.

Fourthly, and ideally, the vision you create in imagining future useful work can feed into the pool of ideas out of which future corporate strategy is formed. A manager was encouraged by a well-designed career and personal development planning process (the one described in Chapter 4) to imagine a totally new job that made sense of his developing skills and trends in the business. The idea passed through into the strategy discussion, was turned into a plan fitted into the strategy, and implemented. This may be unusual; but it can happen.

Fifthly, any option considered in the strategy debate should be evaluated, amongst other things, in terms of whether it can be implemented through the collective management talent of the organization. Strategic options are routinely evaluated in financial, technical and market terms, but too often organizations forget to check managerial viability.

Companies with cash surpluses can diversify primarily on financial logic into areas where they have no ability to manage - and suffer severely for it. Companies can also get into difficulties moving from low to high technology areas where they presume knowledge - say of plastics, glass, building products - failing to appreciate differences involved in managing the production process. You may well have similar experiences.

Management development systems often collect data on the quantity, quality and nature of management talent in an organization to assess the viability of business options without constructing an overall picture. It would be unthinkable for the accounting function to neglect combining departmental budgets into an overall budget - yet management development systems often do exactly this with assessments of managerial competence. It is now argued convincingly that in the era of knowledge work, collective knowledge and competence is becoming the critical factor in organizational survival and prosperity.

Finally, as our understanding of learning develops, and we find new ways of applying it to collective as well as individual work, we have the opportunity to help those involved in the strategy process to change the strategy forming, implementing, evaluation and reviewing process into a learning activity. This is an important aspect of the functioning of a learning company or organization.

2 Burgoyne's Ladder: How Organizations Manage Careers and Development

THE SEVEN LEVELS OF PERFORMANCE

Organizations can be more or less efficient at corporate management development, but by what means could this be simply assessed? This Chapter describes the seven levels of increasingly effective management development. Your organization's current level reflects what goes on 'behind the scenes' of the development and career structuring activities that impact on you directly. Even though the processes themselves may be hidden, their effects should be obvious, so it will be possible for you to make a reasonable judgment about your organization's level.

The levels, summarized in Figure 4 on p.22, are arranged in a stairway or hierarchy. An organization may achieve functioning at any one of the levels, but to do so it must have the lower levels in place (with the exception of level 0). The first to the sixth level indicate the features that are added at each of the corresponding numbered levels. Figure 4 shows the features that accumulate at each level in moving up from 1 to 6. Level 6 therefore has all the features listed, whilst level 1 is characterized by that single feature.

Organizations may climb up this stairway from their inception, but this is not always the case. It is likely to be true of the classic entrepreneurially-driven, small firm that grows. It is less likely to be true of instant, new, larger organizations set up rapidly by sophisticated managers with investment capital, or joint venture companies. Each of these kinds of organizations are likely to start up immediately with sophisticated management systems targeted at the higher levels. Some new organizations may start part of the way up, others may climb and slip back, others may get stuck at

Fig 4: Seven Levels of Functioning of the
Corporate Management Development Process

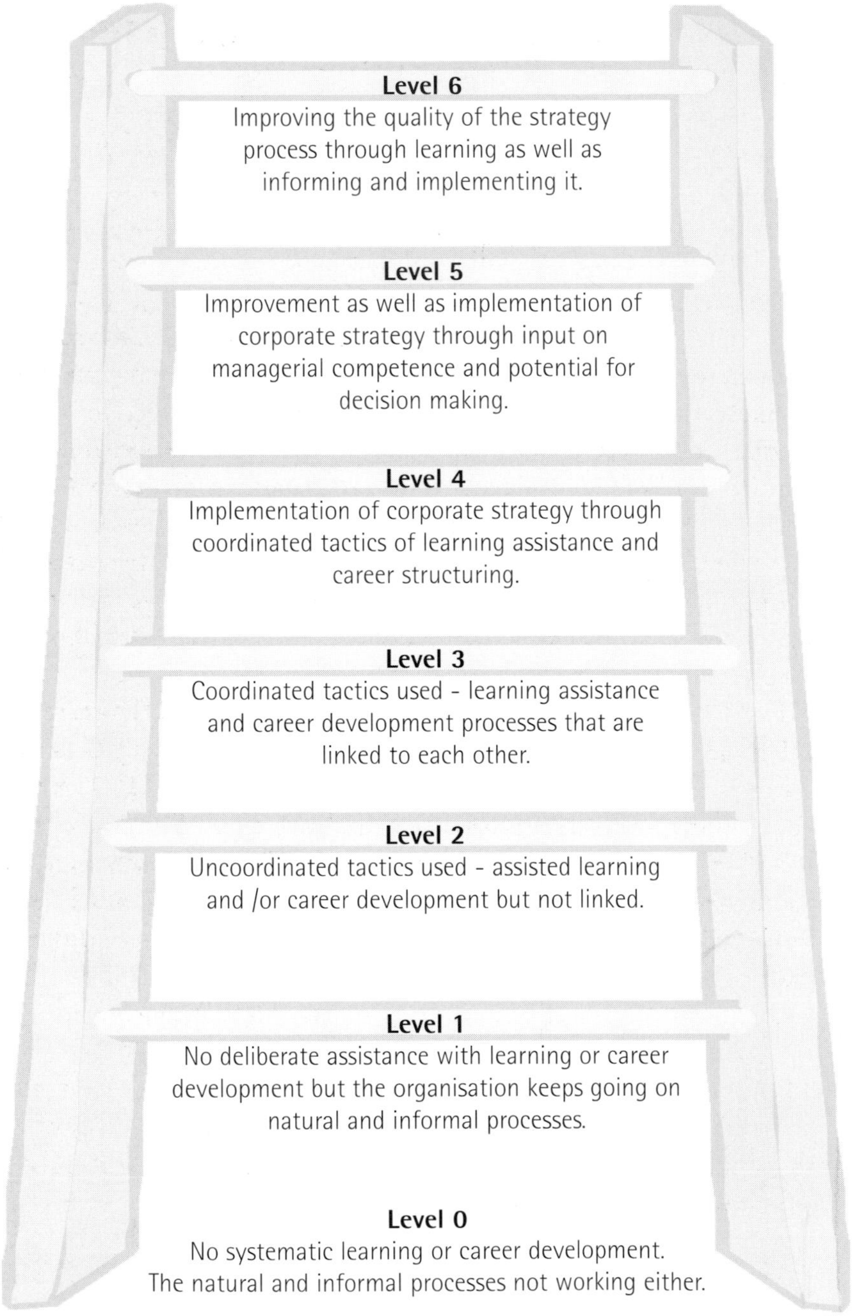

Level 6
Improving the quality of the strategy
process through learning as well as
informing and implementing it.

Level 5
Improvement as well as implementation of
corporate strategy through input on
managerial competence and potential for
decision making.

Level 4
Implementation of corporate strategy through
coordinated tactics of learning assistance and
career structuring.

Level 3
Coordinated tactics used - learning assistance
and career development processes that are
linked to each other.

Level 2
Uncoordinated tactics used - assisted learning
and /or career development but not linked.

Level 1
No deliberate assistance with learning or career
development but the organisation keeps going on
natural and informal processes.

Level 0
No systematic learning or career development.
The natural and informal processes not working either.

one or other of the intermediate levels. This indeed must be the case given the large number of mature organizations to be found in the middle levels.

Describing a new firm climbing the ladder will further explain the model. As previously stated, this may well happen, but is by no means guaranteed. The classic entrepreneurial start-up is likely to be at Level 1. It will be totally preoccupied with applying its start-up idea. It will be small with, at best, a considerable natural learning opportunity as the relatively small number of people involved find themselves in a 'live business game' where all can see what is going on and learn all they need from it. They may well be starting on the basis of foundational skills acquired elsewhere which will keep them going initially. The organization is likely to be informal with the minimum of procedures and flexible roles and role boundaries. Alternatively, the organization may be run by a clear-sighted and charismatic individual who can keep everything for the time being in his or her own head. 'Career moves' will take place very informally. The organization is small enough for everyone to know everyone else and almost everything that goes on. This informal process may not get into serious trouble or miss major opportunities.

Small businesses can however slip back to Level 0 where the informal processes do not work, particularly if early business success does not come easily. In this situation work can become very short term and survival oriented. It is then difficult to stop, reflect and learn. People are likely to step into operations and forget to manage altogether. Such organizations may not last for long, accounting for the distressingly high rate of small business failure in their early years.

★

How are the levels of corporate management development recognized in practice? Here are some typical indications of each level together with some illustrative incidents.

Level 0: No systematic learning

At this basic level no systematic, natural or informal learning or career development is taking place.

Indicative perceptions

- "We are on the brink of collapse and deal with it by working harder."

- "We should stop and think if there is a better way of doing things but there just isn't time."

- "We all do the jobs we have accumulated historically, we could probably do better if we re-sorted them but we can never take the time to do it."

- "I am sure there are skills, techniques, areas of knowledge that would help me work better, but I can never find the time to find and follow up the relevant learning opportunities."

Illustrative incident

Blake's Windows makes windows, doors and window frames for the building trade. They have three assemblers, a delivery driver, a sales/marketing manager, and an operations manager who also does the accounts. They work in a rented factory unit on a trading estate. None of them is particularly happy in their jobs but they are too busy just surviving to think about how to rearrange their ways of working. There are simple planning, accounting and production procedures that their competition use that they are vaguely aware of, which would make them much more efficient, but they never get round to finding out more about them.

Level 1: No deliberate assistance with learning

At this level there is no purposeful assistance with learning or career development, but the organization keeps going on natural and informal processes.

Indicative perceptions

- "I am involved in new activities and learning new things all the time."

- "I can see how the whole organization works as a system."

- "We know each other and each other's work so well we can shift the jobs around between us."

Illustrative incident

Webcraft is an enthusiastic group of website designers who share all their work, and spend an hour every Monday morning and Friday afternoon reviewing their assignments, checking completions, sharing new work, and making sure the invoices go out. They all get better at their work as they try new ideas, find out more about what their clients like, and what they can charge for their work. The trouble is that the staff keep getting recruited for higher pay by their clients, or occasionally branch out on their own and set up in competition with Webcraft.

Small businesses that succeed are likely to grow and reach a stage where not everyone can be noticed. Talent is overlooked if informal career development processes are relied on exclusively. Systems and specialization are likely to become necessary as the organization itself becomes more complicated to run, calling for abilities not needed before.

In addition to this, with the passage of time, founding members may wish to retire or move on. It is not uncommon for them to have been so influential, kept so much in their head, relied so much on their own inspiration and energy, that a succession crisis is created. Nobody else has had enough experience to take over from them.

This situation is a crisis point in the growth of small businesses, and not all of them survive it. Those that do may train within or recruit from outside as a crisis measure. When this happens organizations tend to take steps to prevent it happening again.

Level 2: Uncoordinated tactics

At this level assisted learning and/or career development takes place but it is not linked. The problems associated with Level 1 functioning is often the starting point for Level 2: the appointment or allocation of someone to implement something like succession planning, and possibly to review the stock of available abilities and initiate a training and development programme. This would involve making successors to the occupants of key jobs - perhaps identifying general areas of weakness, for example, project management, entrepreneurialism, cost control - and setting up courses and workshops on these. An appraisal scheme could also be set up to map more systematically the talents of all the managers working in the organization, so that they could be matched to future jobs.

Indicative perceptions

- "I end up on learning events without knowing why I am there."

- "We tend to be 'sheep dipped' in the same courses and programmes whether we need them or not."

- "We occasionally get assessed for our career potential or development needs but there is no follow up."

- "Our performance is measured but we are not helped to improve it."

Illustrative incidents

A small engineering firm grew over the years by doing excellent work of the highest technical quality, and developed an excellent reputation for delivering on time. One year the company went very close to bankruptcy by seriously underestimating the cost of a fixed price contract from which they could not escape. After that the company developed a course in finance, estimating, costing, contracting and cost control for non-financial managers, which all staff attended, and which became part of the induction programme. This accounted for the entire training budget. Some of the people who went on the programme felt they already knew the material; others never had the need or opportunity to apply it. Others felt there were different kinds of expertise they could more usefully develop.

....

A small firm had a crisis when its founder retired. Although this event was known to be coming, no preparations were made, and a head hunting consultant had to be used at the last minute to find a successor from the outside. The head hunting firm persuaded the firm that they should also recruit a director of human resources, who then instituted a succession planning scheme to ensure someone internal was earmarked as a replacement for all key jobs. There was, however, no training or development for the people on the succession lists, and not all of them wanted the jobs they were nominated for when the jobs eventually fell vacant.

Level 2 systematic activities are useful but ad hoc, solving immediate problems and probably preventing them happening again. They survive through habit and inertia, and are uncoordinated.

Sooner or later it becomes apparent that the succession planning is not working as the people designated are not being developed for the jobs they are destined for, and such training that is going on is addressed to historical and not present or future problems. This generates, at best, recognition of the need to coordinate these activities, and to ensure that career formation is linked to learning and development and vice versa. In other words the organization moves to the next level.

Level 3: Coordinated tactics

At this level coordinated tactics are employed so that learning is assisted and career development processes are linked to each other. This is the systematization stage of the management development process, and of the organization in general. It is the growth point in a firm when it is felt that what has been known informally as 'how to do things' needs to be regularized as routine. Principles and procedures are established that ensure development exclusively supports careers.

A characteristic Level 3 problem is when procedures become detached from the process by which the business evolves, changes its strategy, or goes through regular change and restructuring. Most commonly, Level 3 concentrates on replacing existing skills rather than developing new ones, and conducts career planning on the assumption that the basic structure of the organization will stay more or less the same.

In many organizations where change programmes are introduced at times of crisis after periods of lack of adaptation, highly complex Level 3 management development systems become obsolete overnight as the world people have been prepared for through career planning and development disappears. There is obviously a large material and human cost to such events.

Indicative perceptions

- "I understand the processes and procedures through which my career might develop in this organization - whether through planning or an internal market where I can apply for jobs. The systems are clear and on the whole can be seen to be working."

- "Where career reviews, performance appraisals, and so on lead to the identification of something I should learn, it is clear who is responsible for following this up and making it happen."

- "When I do get involved in courses or programmes for learning there is shared and accepted understanding of what I should learn."

But...

- "The skills and competencies I have the opportunity to develop are based on those that are effective today, and have ensured success for people today, rather than those forecast to be important in the future."

- "Career and succession discussions and planning is based on the assumption that the main jobs, posts and roles that exist now will also exist in the future."

Illustrative incidents

Typical answers given by managers evaluating and assessing their experience on training course programmes that suggest Level 3 functioning are:

- I think they send everyone at my level sooner or later.

- My boss was supposed to come, but something urgent came up, so I am here rather than waste the place.

- The department had to meet its training days' target by the end of the year, and it was my turn.

- I think we had to spend the training budget by the end of the financial year.

- The message came round that the managing director wanted to see the programme full, and I was the only one with the dates free in my diary.

Organizations that foresee such problems or endure and survive them, or are persuaded to take on initiatives like the UK's Investors in People Scheme (which audits organizations on their ability to demonstrate training schemes that implement new corporate strategy), may move to Level 4. At this level career planning and development are informed by and used to implement new and emergent strategies and structures.

Level 4: Implementing policy

At this level corporate strategy is implemented through coordinated tactics of learning assistance and career structuring.

Level 4 functioning might be regarded as the absolute minimum requirement for a mature organization operating in a changing and competitive environment. Unfortunately, all too many contemporary organizations only achieve Level 4 sporadically and for short periods when they restructure and reorganize. They then appear to revert to Levels 3 or 2, until the inertia that this implies builds up pressure or a crisis to precipitate the next reorganization and revert to Level 4 functioning.

Some organizations survive this way - others do not - failing at one or other of the attempted reorganizations. Those that survive appear to do so by shrinking in each successive wave of change. Many managers in and out of work, are the casualties of organizations that treated them for long periods according to Level 2 and 3 processes, only to disrupt their careers and development in panic episodes of Level 4 functioning.

Organizations that are able to function at Level 4 more

continuously avoid the worst of the organizational and individual costs incurred in this erratic process. Level 4 functioning on a sustained basis allows continuous adaptation that should be less costly and crisis-ridden in the long term.

Indicative perceptions

- "When new strategies and structures are announced we are invited to say which of the new jobs we think we could do, and are considered for them."

- "We are told about possible changes in the business so that we can see the directions the business might take in the future."

- "We have support in finding and using all kinds of training opportunities to keep ourselves up to date."

- "We have meetings in which we share what we have learnt in making new business processes work."

Illustrative incident

A firm that has now become one of the UK's 'big five' consultancy firms transformed itself some years ago from being mainly an accountancy audit service. The strategic logic was driven on the one hand by the declining profitability of the basic auditing business and on the other by critical insight into their clients' businesses derived from auditing the accounts. The structure of the firm had been predominantly cell-like teams of accountants with their own sets of clients. The new strategy required a structure of various groups of consulting specialists - IT, operations management, human resource planning, corporate strategy, marketing, and so on - to which clients could be referred for help. The role of auditors therefore had to be expanded to provide an initial 'diagnosis' of organizational problems and opportunities in order to make appropriate referrals.

To achieve all this, new structures and roles were introduced. Careers were renegotiated with existing staff. Some stayed, some became redundant; new staff were recruited. An elaborate development programme was introduced to assist all these people understand and become effective in this new scheme. The programme ranged from general briefings to specific skills workshops to participation in consortial MBA courses with the twin objective of developing broad managerial skills, having more qualified teams, and integrating the experience of working with managers from a broad spectrum of organizations and industries.

This illustration shows how a new strategic vision and plan is followed through and implemented by coordinated tactics of re-planning careers and supporting people with development programmes to assist them fit their new roles. These are the processes that are the essence of Level 4.

Level 5: Improving and implementing policy

At this level improvement as well as implementation of corporate strategy is made through input on managerial competence and potential for decision making.

Organizations functioning at Level 4 can still make mistakes in strategy through choosing directions that are not viable in managerial terms, without being aware of this in advance. Without input from corporate management development into strategy formation to assess the organization's ability to manage a proposed new direction, as well as an output from strategy to direct its implementation through management development, there is a greatly increased risk of committing the organization to plans that management cannot implement. Level 5 is defined by the addition of this input. This means that corporate management development maintains a picture of the overall managerial capability of the organization so that it can evaluate the ease or difficulty, time-scale and cost of setting up and running managerial processes for any proposed new venture. It may further be able to contribute to new ideas by asking what organizational and business directions would make best use of the organization's managerial capability - such ideas can then be checked out for financial, technical and market viability.

Illustrative perceptions

- "New policies and strategies do seem to take into account my own special talents and those of my colleagues."

- "Where new projects require new knowledge and skills they are accompanied by plans to train us in them or add them to our teams by recruiting people with the new kinds of skills."

- "My ideas about how our work is changing, what opportunities are emerging for us, what special expertise we have to exploit, get a serious hearing and can influence what we do."

Illustrative incident

The board meets to discuss strategy and to identify new business ventures to follow. The technical director reports on the company's leading-edge technology, new patents, latest research and state of the art production arrangements, and suggests opportunities arising from this. The marketing director assesses the potential of the brand to promote new products and services, the potential for new business in the customer base, and the competitive advantage of the company's selling and distribution system. The finance director describes the company's ability to put risk capital into new ventures. We can say that Level 5 has been achieved if the human resources director is able to describe the core managerial competence of the company, point out business opportunities that arise from this; is able to say whether the organization has the managerial ability, both qualitatively and quantitatively, to put into practice any new business idea - or say what it would take in time and money to recruit and train managers, and is sufficiently informed by human resources information systems to be able to do this. Unfortunately, not many organizations appear to achieve Level 5 functioning in a sustained way. Those that do derive considerable advantage - making few big business mistakes, changing continuously rather than sporadically, and sustaining this performance for long periods.

Level 5, as I will explain in more detail later, is the minimum for an organization to be able to function as a learning company or organization. In essence, this is because the two-way process between management development policy and corporate strategy allows for the necessary linkage between individual and organizational learning.

Level 6: The learning organization

At the final level the quality of the strategy process is improved through learning as well as informing and implementing it. What we know about learning is added to the strategy process itself and the people involved in making it - (represented by the outside line, labelled 6 in Figure 3 on p. 16). Strategy formation is pursued as a learning process both collectively and for those involved in its formulation. Strategy is experimental and effort is made to learn quickly from its implementation to obtain maximum learning from the minimum risk, and then to move rapidly to take advantage of lessons learnt. This mode of operating takes a business fully into the strategic functioning of a learning company or organization.

If a new idea comes up, in a strategy discussion, the immediate response is not "that's a great idea" or "that would never work" but "how can we try that out to see if it is as good as it sounds".

When a new project is being implemented, there is enthusiasm but not blind faith. People ask: "How will we know as soon as possible whether it is working or not? What are our success criteria? What are the earliest measures we can take to see if it is working, and identify corrective action if necessary? With what evidence and under what circumstances would we be convinced that the project should be abandoned?"

Illustrative perceptions

- "When new strategies and projects are adopted we are clear about what we expect to learn together as an organization from pursuing them."

- "With new projects and strategies we agree the indicators that will show if they are working or need adapting, and we use them."

- "New ideas are not instantly accepted or condemned but considered in terms of how they can be tried out experimentally."

Illustrative incident

Westfield Leisure Services develops its potential senior managers by having them work in task forces on projects identified by the board as being the key strategic issues for the future of the firm. The board demands analysis and proposals from the task groups. For ideas that they judge to be promising they ask for a business plan and when these are judged as feasible the task forces can become full-time teams to implement the plans.

Applying the 'Ladder' Model to Parts and Sub-Parts of an Organization

This way of thinking has assumed or imagined 'the organization' or 'the company' as a relatively straightforward entity. Reality is rather more complicated. For example, Radio Rentals is a UK retail company forming part of the domestic products division of Thorn EMI - which also has other divisions, like music, with companies that, for example, collect royalties for music played on radio stations around the world. If you are a manager in Radio Rentals which organization do you work for? Radio Rentals or all of them? If a complex organization like this has a coherent approach to management development it will be clear what happens at company, division and corporate level, and what is standardized and what is devolved to appropriate local structures.

What is on the other end of your formal and psychological contract of employment? A formal contract of employment has a legal entity attached to it. Do you know what it is for you? As your primary employer, you should think about what formal systems it has. For example, if it is part of a larger set-up, then there may be systems to encourage inter-divisional career mobility that you might want to know about and consider using.

In terms of the psychological contract, what is it that you feel you belong to? To what do you feel loyalty and commitment? Is it the department or unit, or the company or corporation? Within what domain do you seem to have career opportunities? It is worth thinking these things through, and considering the relation between the formal and psychological contract. In these days of out-sourcing, subcontracting and rationalization, it is not unusual for managers working for blue chip companies to find themselves transferred as their department is cut loose or sold off to a supply company. This could be exciting and challenging, or it could be exploitative and depressing - it is better to think of these things ahead, and be prepared for the opportunities and threats they bring.

Evidence for the effectiveness of the model

The ladder model can be justified on rational and logical ground; companies that are better in these terms are also more profitable. This is a practical rather than a research book, but there is firm evidence to support the view that companies that have the more integrated approaches to management development implied by the higher stages of the model perform better financially - as measured by rate of return on capital employed set against averages for the company's industries.

A study that covered about 50 companies investigated retrospectively over a period of up to 10 years highlighted a number of interesting facts. Firstly, there was a considerable degree of variation on how much the systems implied in the model were formalized into overt procedures or operated through clear but less systematized custom and practice. There was no evidence that either was better than the other in terms of outcome. Secondly, many companies have some of the features of Levels 5 and 6 but without the full infrastructure that Levels 1 to 4 imply. This suggests that although it is useful to think of companies working at one or other of the levels, there may also be situations that are better understood as partial working at the different stages.

CHOOSING YOUR PERSONAL STRATEGY IN THE LIGHT OF YOUR ORGANIZATION'S LEVEL

Whatever the level of any organization you do or might work for, you can probably make it work at a higher level for you. If you are on the receiving end of career potential assessment or assessment centres, you can ask what development follow-up you can have or expect. When you find yourself on a course or involved in any other planned learning process, you can ask what it is for and how it fits with career planning or opportunities. If you can think of useful and fulfilling jobs that you might do, but which do not exist, you can suggest these. You can ask what re-structurings are in the pipeline and what big issues and uncertainties exist about strategies and structures for the future, as background to thinking about your own future career possibilities.

It is a useful exercise to make a list of the stakeholders in your career and personal development - for example, line managers, colleagues, local and central personnel/human resources people and so on. Then talk to them about what you are and should be learning, and the kinds of work that you might find or have the opportunity to do in the future.

Most organizations of any size have specialists who deal with career and management development. You may know who they are and what they do, or you could find out with a little research. They may have formal titles involving 'management education', 'training', or 'development', or they may be labelled human resource managers/developers, employee relations advisers, or organization development specialists. They may offer systematic services, or run systematic processes or they may work as internal consultants on various one-off initiatives.

If you behave assertively about your development it is more likely than not that this will be welcomed and encouraged by the management development specialists who will welcome the grass roots support for improving the efficiency of what they are trying to do.

Consider how you could use these people and the systems they operate. They are a resource to help you, they should be interested in you, keen to help, and appreciative of your intelligent interest in what they are trying to do. Activity 9 on p.117 will help you assess how much you know about these specialists.

3 Understanding and Using Corporate Career Development Processes

This chapter is about the structural side of career development. Organizations use a variety of methods and procedures to manage and influence the way people are recruited into and move about between roles and jobs, and meet collective needs and serve emergent strategic priorities. In the process they hopefully use individual talents and give people careers that are satisfying and rewarding. The chapter helps you understand what some of these methods are so you can understand better how your career is formed, and how to act as an intelligent partner in this process. It contains no exercises as such, but as you read it you will no doubt reflect on the kinds of career structuring methods you have witnessed and the predominant ones in your current circumstances.

It is helpful to know the standard kinds of practices that organizations use these days to structure careers. This involves knowing and understanding the terms, and working out which are the ones mainly used in any organization you work for. As each one is a mechanism for career negotiation between you and your organization/employer, the more you understand the better the negotiation.

The methods to be covered are: *succession planning* - the practice of identifying likely successors to all jobs, or key jobs; *fast track schemes* - special cohorts of people recruited or internally selected for special programmes of experience and development; *assessment centres* - events to assess suitability and potential for future work (and often development as well); *psychometric measurement* - a set of technologies to measure abilities, skills and personality as an input to selection/placement decisions; and *head hunting* (*internal and external*) - the practice of conducting specific searches for people to fill a specific job. There are also specific methods that are broader approaches, like creating *open and semi-open internal labour marketplaces* - the practice of inviting applications for jobs internally.

In addition to these formally designed and set up processes there are informal processes and evolved practices which are as or sometimes more influential in determining who actually gets to do what: *seniority, family allegiances, networks, clubs, clans and professional groupings*. Even more informal and often invisible are *cultural beliefs, stories and myths* about career progression which determine unconscious mindsets within which employment decisions are framed and made.

Finally, as many organizations become or aspire to be more global, international, cross-nationally located in business networks and respond to moral and legal frameworks on employment, then career moves and choices are subject to *cross national differences, ethnic and gender issues, equal opportunity, anti-discriminatory, difference and diversity policies and programmes*.

SUCCESSION PLANNING

At its simplest succession planning is the process of taking an organization chart and asking who would fill each post if that person were to leave. This process generates a succession list for each job. There are many variations in the application of this principle. It can be done for most posts or only for those judged as critical. It can be done openly, so that the results are visible to all, or secretly so that almost no one knows about it. It can be done by personnel professionals or by line managers. People can be chosen for lists on intuition or judgment or through information from a whole range of systematic procedures. Succession lists can be formally written down, or stored in tailored software packages, or remain informal, existing as 'understandings' amongst key senior managers. Finally, succession lists can be arrived at unilaterally - without much or any discussion with those concerned - or through negotiation and discussion with the potential successors.

For human resource management, succession planning is advantageous in that it identifies problem situations: key posts with no obvious successors; a small handful of employees expected to replace key posts in the company; or another group of people considered unsuitable for any other post. Succession planning lists can be made sophisticated by reaching across from the structural to the developmental side, by saying that each person on a succession list should have a development plan to prepare them for the post to which they might succeed.

Succession planning belongs to an 'organization-centred', as opposed to a 'self-driven and free internal labour market' approach. This means, at the extreme, the organization is staffed as a result of central decisions as opposed to vacant posts being advertised openly. There has been a trend in the 1980s and 1990s towards the open market approach, signalling a decline in succession planning. Yet the open market approach may be more talk than reality in some organizations, and in others where it has been used, findings suggest that too much free market input leaves the organization vulnerable to the loss or sub-optimal use of talent. With the growing awareness that organizations are increasingly involved in 'knowledge work' - the need to keep people as key assets should see a return to career practices that manage careers more directively.

You need to reflect on whether you are working in a context where there is any form of succession planning which incorporates your own orientation and your own possible response. You may have opportunities to discuss or even consent to succession lists and to discuss and follow development plans to support this. The processes may be more secretive or informal or they may exist patchily or outside your domain. You may find yourself in informal networks or have understandings and relationships with former bosses that amount to succession expectations. You may be aware of other people, but not yourself, being in such situations.

If you do not know what is happening, asking is the easiest way to find out. You will know of the micro-politics and local cultural acceptability of doing this, and the way to do it, or if not you might learn by trying.

Another approach is to identify some other job in your setting that you might genuinely aspire to do, and to find out how such posts get filled and how the system works both formally and informally. You might get the job or at least encourage greater interest in your career and personal development, and you are certain to find out more about how your organization works.

FAST TRACK SCHEMES

Fast track schemes occur when selected groups of managers or trainee managers are managed, from a career and development perspective, as a special set of people. These can take the form of early career schemes such as - graduate trainee schemes (considered necessary to attract the 'best' graduates). There can also be middle or late career stage fast track schemes.

The generally accepted, or at least stated, rationale for such schemes is that jobs in today's complex organizations require experiences that people do not get if normal processes are left to run their course. Hence, this special experience - across functions, disciplines and business areas, together with specific training and development - is managed for them. It is difficult to judge whether such functional and meritocratic rationales can be taken as genuine, or whether such schemes are mechanisms by which elites look after themselves - a question that is beyond the scope of this book.

The alternative to fast track schemes, is surprisingly - no fast track scheme - a more self and market-oriented approach, somewhat Darwinian, in which the system is trusted or designed to enable people to evolve their own careers, experience and skills to fill all necessary posts. Critics of fast track schemes point out that however motivating and rewarding they are for participants, organizations may pay a high cost through the effect they have on those excluded. In an uncertain world, doubt must be cast on the implied assumption that performance and potential are predictable decades in advance.

Fast track schemes can vary greatly in their size relative to the overall managerial population, the job experience mix, the amount of training and development, the 'realness' of the jobs and whether and how people can leave or join the scheme. They can also vary in their degree of internal streaming and in the amount of competitiveness engendered within them through assessment and league-tabling of members.

Some organizations have more than one scheme - corporate and divisional, or special ones for some professional categories. Often there is variety and even confusion as result of schemes being changed, so that different cohorts work on different designs. Or organizations can be merged, acquired, taken over, de-merged or bought out and have a variety of schemes running either wholeheartedly or in atrophied forms. Fast track schemes, even when discontinued, can leave powerful cultural and informal traces, such as loyal networks of ex-members who either do, or are seen to, look after each other and who have strong and sometimes influential views on what is good for the development of others.

It is useful to understand your context. You may be on a scheme, outside one, have the opportunity to join one or be somewhere where there are none. It is at least worth knowing and taking a view on the opportunities and constraints that the system in your context gives you. If you consider moving between organizations be aware of the great variety of practices that exist between organizations.

Finally, it is worth noting there is another kind of semi-formal fast track, which takes place between organizations, within and between industries. Some 'blue chip' companies act, deliberately or not, as training and career development grounds for their whole industry. Depending on your age and aspirations you might want to think about your context in these terms. There are also emergent 'fast track career routes', such as moving from business school to multi-national consultancy firm to a senior job with a major client, which are becoming increasingly common.

ASSESSMENT CENTRES

Assessment centres measure people so they can be 'fitted' to current or potential jobs. They are usually specific events involving a mixture of observed simulated task performance, interviews of various kinds, psychometric testing, and possibly other organizationally generated information like performance appraisal. Assessment centres can also be presented as developmental with a logic of diagnosis and feedback that is claimed to support and lay the foundations for development. Assessment and development centres can be taken at face value as measures for career placement purposes and initiators of development, or interpreted as assertions of organizational power in the career bargaining process. They can be seen as powerful reminders to the individual that the organization appraises, judges and places them, and may serve to pass a cultural message and maintain a sense of personal competitiveness between colleagues.

Again, understand what is happening around you. Work out how assessment centres operate in the dynamics of your organization and how you want to use them. Do not be overawed by them, or believe any sense of scientific objectivity they create about knowing your personality. None of the tools and methods they use justify this. Use them as positive opportunities to present yourself as you want to be seen, and to get what you want.

PSYCHOMETRIC MEASUREMENT

Psychometric measurement is a methodology much used in assessment centres. It is based on the assumption and assertion that aspects of people - personality, attitudes, skills, abilities, competencies, preferences and values - can be measured relatively reliably and scientifically and, furthermore, that these things are predictive or determining of job fit and performance. These methods are widely used and indeed represent an enormous industry in themselves. However, even by their own logic they are rarely if ever used in a full-blown scientific way, which would require a given test for a job being proved by research to be predictive of performance in that job. Virtually all applications make an act of faith that some test can be useful in a selection placement situation, or else that they are 'an input to a human judgment process'. Yet their scale of use is not justified by scientific evidence of accuracy.

It is tempting therefore to make another interpretation - that their use is meant to intimidate and control, to imply that the organization knows more about you than you do yourself, and that you must subject yourself to a rational organizational process beyond your control. This may be an extreme interpretation but you should not be overawed by psychometric tests, or feel dissempowered by a belief that others have a special knowledge of you to which you do not have access. Do not be convinced there are fixed things about you that determine where you fit. Assert that you have choice about what you are like. It is certainly true that some people believe, counter to the view of psychometrics, that the testee can and does choose how to present themselves through the tests. And why not?

It is true, however, that many people find the results of their own tests interesting and useful. The categories and descriptions they use do offer new ways of thinking about yourself. Use them to think about options that you have or habits you may have got into, rather than declarations of fixed characteristics that decide your fate.

Person-by-person competency databases are an extension of some of the methods discussed. Data on you and your competencies can be kept, along with those of others, on a database to identify people for jobs and assignments. Organizations that attempt this achieve limited use. However, they are rarely if ever used as the only identification process. It is doubtful if people can ever be measured enough to make it really work, and there are practical problems of collecting all the information and keeping it up to date. If you work in an organization with such a system it may provide an opportunity to be logged as having skills and interests you want to use and pursue.

INTERNAL AND EXTERNAL HEAD HUNTING

Head hunting arose initially as a mode of external recruitment in which someone is approached to fill a job. It is usually a personal process in which the head hunter profiles an area to locate people with a good reputation who may not be particularly looking for a new job or job change. Some agencies keep lists on which you can include yourself if you are interested in being considered or approached. Some of these approaches are sometimes used within large complex organizations.

You should recognize that reputation and visibility affect career prospects. This seems perhaps an obvious observation though not one acknowledged in practice. It is worth considering what your reputation is - good and bad, what creates it and who is aware of it.

OPEN AND SEMI-OPEN INTERNAL LABOUR MARKET PLACES

The open labour market approach has already been mentioned. In organizational settings this translates into policies and practices where jobs are openly advertised within organizations so that anyone has the right and opportunity to apply. Of course, where these principles are applied individuals can and are encouraged (or discouraged) from applying with varying degrees of force, and whoever recruits can be highly selective about who they take. But the principle is one of open application. For some organizations this offers an attractive alternative between jobs for life and fixed term-job employment. In effect, the psychological contract can be stated as, 'You have got a job with us, you are a member of the family, we make you no guarantees of a career but you have the opportunity and our support in finding a career for yourself through the open jobs market.'

Organizations that do work this way should make job awareness easy - through using computerized databases, especially in organizations where a large proportion of staff work through networked PCs. Equally, such organizations should offer development opportunities under user control, enabling development for the kinds of jobs the users want to apply for. This is often delivered through learning resource centres, open programmes and processes of self-nomination for learning events. If you are in this kind of situation you have the opportunity to follow your own plan of self-development to prepare you for the kinds of jobs you foresee and would like to apply for.

INFORMAL AND TRADITIONAL PROCESSES

This covers processes derived from seniority, family allegiances, networks, clubs and clans, professional groupings. It is worth noting that the formal logic of most Western, Anglo-American and many European organizations is based on the combined principles of rational management planning, meritocratic competition and intended fairness over non-performance related features - gender, age, race, ethnicity and religion. It is recognised that, for better or worse, informal practices sometimes diverge from this as do formal ones - particularly seniority rights. However, there are some cultures and parts of the world where nepotism is the normal and culturally-accepted way of doing things.

CULTURAL BELIEFS, STORIES AND MYTHS

Most or all organizations have their myths, beliefs and stories about what actually shapes careers. A high proportion of the rumour systems of organizations are directly and indirectly about careers. Myths have the property of becoming self fulfilling. A common myth is the belief that if you refuse a new job opportunity you will never get offered another one. Human resources professionals often collude with or encourage such myths to give them power needed to fill jobs that are unpopular because of what they are, who they are with, or where they are. It is worth being aware of your organization's cultural beliefs on careers, and to avoid either being controlled by them or getting into difficulty by patently ignoring them.

CULTURAL, INTERNATIONAL AND OTHER INFLUENCES

The career practices of all organizations are influenced by national and international employment laws and principles that seek to create fairness of various kinds and encourage diversity of employment on several dimensions. Many organizations have their own additional policies where actual implementation adheres to greater or lesser degrees to their expressed principles and could cover cross-national differences, ethnic and gender issues, equal opportunity, anti-discriminatory, difference and diversity policies and programmes. You should be aware of these policies and practices both in general and as they affect your rights, obligations and opportunities. Sometimes people have to be assertive to the extent of using legal mechanisms to achieve their rights.

4 Using Learning Opportunities

The way we learn most of the time is like the way we stay healthy. Fortunately much of the time we stay healthy naturally and likewise most of us learn all the time, though the more so if we are doing work where there is scope to experiment, explore, try things out, compare ideas and experiences with others. Occasionally we need help, or to make a special effort ourselves, to move into a new area of achievement or to deal with some persistent difficulty. Just as there is a tendency to equate health with going to the doctor, so there is a tendency to equate learning with being taught or trained. Being taught, trained, or going to the doctor has much to offer us but we miss a lot if we limit ourselves to this mindset. Learning is anything that enables you to become clearer about what you want to do, and better at doing it. Formal education, training and development is only a small, though important, part of this.

You will remember that in Activity 7 you were asked to explore how you actually learnt some of the current abilities you rely on. Activity 10 on p.118 is a further opportunity to consider how you learn.

A ACTIVITY 10 Page 118

Whether you are trying to optimize what you get from informal, on-the-job learning, or more formal, systematic training, education or development, it helps to have some idea about how you learn so that you can make best use of the opportunities.

There are many theories and models of learning, many recommended teaching and learning methods, and principles that can be followed. Unfortunately, there are few if any universal truths about learning. How you learn appears to depend on your personality, what you are learning, the situation you are in and your history. We all have a variety of learning processes that we use, many of which we are not aware. The more we know of different ways of understanding the learning process, the more we can choose our own strategies, and make the best use of informal and formal learning opportunities to be what we want to be.

FORMAL LEARNING OPPORTUNITIES

Formal learning opportunities often present themselves to you as methods and packages. It helps to be aware of the variety of these so that you have as broad a range of choice as possible. Some of the main ones are described below.

Courses and programmes - events that may themselves use a variety of methods.

Mentoring is a process in which a person with more experience pays special attention to helping you learn from your work experience with their advice.

Coaching provides one-to-one assistance in developing a specific skill or in dealing with a particular type of situation.

Open and distance learning - a generic type to label learning opportunities intended to be as convenient as possible in terms of time, place, access, entry requirements and processes, the pace at which you study, how you learn and the kind of support you draw on.

Actual and virtual learning resource centres - where there are a number of learning resources available, largely of a self-study nature, for you to choose and use. Like a library with packages, tapes and computer programmes in addition to books, in virtual form they are available electronically over a network rather than in a physical room.

Action Learning - in which you are helped, often in a small group meeting with an action learning set adviser, to learn as much as possible from taking action in your work situation, observing the consequences, thinking about why you do things the way you do and discussing your interpretations with others.

Self-development and self-managed learning - which systematizes the idea that you manage your own learning by providing a structure and suggesting processes in which you set your own learning goals, decide how to achieve them, attempt to do so and evaluate the outcome.

Shadowing - in which you follow, observe and talk with someone who is doing a job you want to learn to do.

Attachments and secondments - in which you work in some setting other than your normal one to broaden and share your experience.

Interactive video and CD Roms - machine-based methods that show and tell you things, give you choices to explore, test you, give you feedback and explore your choices in simulated situations.

Floor coaching is the idea that someone comes to you when you need help in learning to deal with a problem in a new situation - a coach on call, for example, to deal with a new organizational procedure or IT package.

Case studies - where learning comes from reading and discussing real or realistic stories of work situations, projects and problems.

Organizational visits - best thought of as live case studies.

Critical incidents - miniature case studies of incidents that are seen as highly critical or important in their implications.

Simulations and business games - artificial situations intended to simulate an actual work situation where you act and see the consequences of action.

Role playing - physically acting out a different role from your normal one.

STYLES AND WAYS OF LEARNING

Learning varies with what we want to learn and with who we are. We have different learning styles and can use different learning strategies and skills to become better at learning itself.

Some learning events will work for you because their methods and approaches fit with your preferred ways of learning, others will not. Participation will help you to understand your own approach to learning, and the range of learning approaches you are comfortable with. It will also help you to evaluate a learning event and interpret its in-built learning approach. This all contributes to an informal choice about how to proceed with your learning.

There are many ways of thinking about learning. One is that you can learn in three ways; by *input* - being told or shown something; through *discovery* - taking action and seeing what the consequences are; and as a result of *reflection* - considering all the experiences that we have had, all the ideas that we have been exposed to, making personal sense of situations, and classifying what is achieved by different types of actions in different situations - see Figure 5 on page 53.

Fig 5: Three Forms of Learning

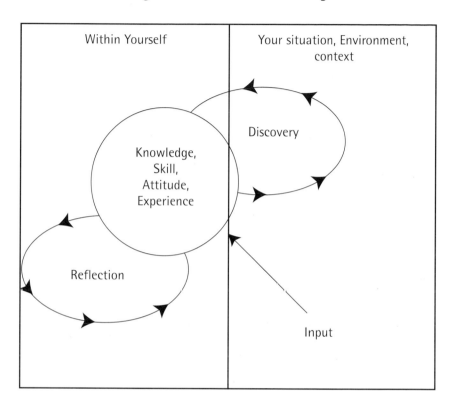

Another way is to think of learning in relation to any given situation, problem, task or opportunity. You have a choice of taking a dependent view or independent view. Taking a *dependent* view means that there is some truth, some tried, tested and proved procedure for dealing with the problem, which you can learn from an expert. An *independent* view means that the situation is unique, that no fixed rule applies to it or at least has yet to be found and that you have to find an approach to it yourself. There is of course a large middle ground between these two extremes, which can be called interdependent, taking the view that while the situation has unique properties there may be knowledge, attitudes or general theories that can be applied from other situations. This dimension represents a choice of attitude that we all make

Fig 6: Learning Attitude to Expertise

DEPENDENT

'There is some truth or tried and tested solution to this problem – finding it is the right approach to learning for this situation.'

INTERDEPENDENT

'This situation is special, however there may be ideas, experiences, practices that have been tried out in similar situations that may help me understand and deal with this one.'

INDEPENDENT

'The problem and situation I am facing here is unique, and I will have to work out for myself what is going on and invent a special way of dealing with it.'

consciously or unconsciously as we try to learn to deal with situations. The whole spectrum may be useful to us in different situations - but remember that, as argued in Chapter 1 management problems are distinct in being unprogrammed. Figure 6 on p.54 shows this range of attitudes.

These two ways of thinking about learning can be combined into a 3 x 3 grid to show your options in any learning situation. See Figure 7 on p.56.

It is tempting to think that all input style learning relates to the dependent attitude, and all discovery learning to the independent attitude, but this is misleading. Some forms of input, for example more educational (rather than training) lecturing is about exploring issues, developing creative and critical perspectives on issues rather than communicating simple truths. Yet at least some discovery learning situations, particularly simulations, are set up to prove a very definite point, or to give practice in very specific and clearly formulated skills.

Fig7: Attitudes To Learning in Formal Situations

		LEARNING MODE	
	Input	Discovery	Reflection
Independent	I will hear about and see ideas, applications and values, and decide which, if any, to adopt for myself.	I expect to have the opportunity to try out different ways of acting, have new experiences, draw new conclusions for myself.	I will work out for myself what is true, workable and valuable, using the suggestions of others.
Interdependent	I will hear about new ideas, procedures and beliefs, and work out with teachers, colleagues which to follow.	I will try things out with others and work out with them what the conclusions are.	I will use the insights of others to make sense of my experiences.
Dependent	I will be told or shown what is true as a theory, what will work as a skill or procedure, what is right morally and ethically.	I expect to be able to demonstrate their effectiveness, and have experiences that show how things work.	I will be guided to an understanding of the truths and patterns behind my experiences.

LEARNING ATTITUDE

5 Strategies and Procedures Linking Learning and Career Development

You will recall that for organizations at Level 3 or above in the 'ladder' model, action to help you learn is coordinated with steps to arrange your career moves. At Level 4 this takes into account what is known and what is uncertain about the future of the organization. At Level 5, ideas arising from new learning or career discussions contribute to deciding future strategies and structures. This means that if you are helped to learn something there is a reasonable understanding of what it is, why you need it and whether it supports you in the short term in your current work or in the long term, in thinking of future work.

Conversely at Level 3 if your fit or performance in current or future work is under consideration, attention is also paid to how learning might improve this fit. For Level 4 your career options and what you can learn are informed both by known changes - new jobs and work phased in as part of agreed new plans - and areas of uncertainty about future organizational activities, structures and work. Preparation for uncertainty may involve learning broad skills and areas of knowledge, developing the ability to learn itself and broadening yourself to take on a broad range of possible emergent jobs and roles. At Level 5, career discussions may throw up ideas for future work based on your actual and potential abilities. Or, projects carried out in training and development events - working on current organizational problems as live case studies - may lead to business ideas which bring new kinds of work through their implementation.

Sometimes organizations have management development mechanisms specifically aimed at creating the link between career development processes and learning opportunities and events. If this applies to your context it is useful to understand and make best use of them. If it does not, you can still work to create some of these processes for yourself. The usual way in which this linkage is made is either through building out from career tactics or by the process in which you choose or are sent on a learning event.

Annual or periodic appraisal systems usually focus primarily on current performance, but they may include discussions of career potential, competencies for the future as well as the present and what you could to learn through a 'personal development plan'. In some organizations there are formal mechanisms for following up development needs identified in this way. Equally, though less frequently, the process of nomination, selection, attendance and choice for courses and learning events may include some relatively systematic process of working out what and why you need to learn, and how it will benefit your work and career path in the short and long term.

If you work in a context with these kinds of mechanisms you can actively use them to form and implement your own career and development plan. If they do not exist you can use the underlying idea to raise questions and make requests about learning and career development opportunities.

An example follows of a corporate scheme for integrating career development and learning that shows how this idea can work. It may help you in identifying and using similar processes and it also suggests processes that you could use 'unilaterally' to take an initiative in managing your own career and development wherever you work. The example is followed by Activity 11, designed to assist you to work out some career scenarios and a personal development plan.

*

A number of years ago I helped to design and implement a career and development planning process in the research and development organization at Esso in Abingdon, England. It was designed mainly for the key professional researchers and research leaders who were expensive to employ and support and who worked on projects critical to current and future business activities. It was generally recognized that 'mistakes' in the development and career placing of these individuals were very expensive in direct costs and probably even more expensive in lost opportunities.

A workbook was written which helped the user, through a series of exercises, to develop some possible career scenarios for their future, and, in a second stage, a personal development plan. Figure 8 on p.60 shows the workbook cover, which illustrates the structure and logic of how the exercises - outlined below - take the user through the process portrayed metaphorically as a chemical plant.

The Rational Skills Tester (1) is a warm-up activity with a few exercises to test reasoning skills that might also help the user identify an area of new learning. The workbook is structured for the user to accumulate a list of areas in which they could possibly usefully learn - the 'Crude Learning Objectives' vat (2) in Figure 8.

The first serious exercise is the Current Skills/Job Matcher (3) where the user simply writes two lists: the skills they have and the skills their current work demands. Skills the person does not have but that the work demands obviously contribute likely learning goals. Skills the person has but is not using, are used as a starting point for the user to think how these skills could be utilized in future work. The next two exercises are about the future. The World Trend Predictor (4) asks the user to imagine how the world of work opportunities might change for them. It asks them to spot technical, social, economic, political and market trends and to imagine what their world of work might be like in the future. The Personal Life Goal Sorter (5), concerned with personal priorities and motives, asks the user what they get from their work and to consider how this might change. The next exercise - the Career Plan Generator (6) - brings together ideas from the previous ones and concludes the first phase.

The user is asked to sketch two or three possible career scenarios, taking into account the trends, personal desires and skills they have explored. It is left to the user to decide how to do this, but it is suggested they might vary them in terms of being

Fig 8: A schematic map of a
collaborative career and development planning system

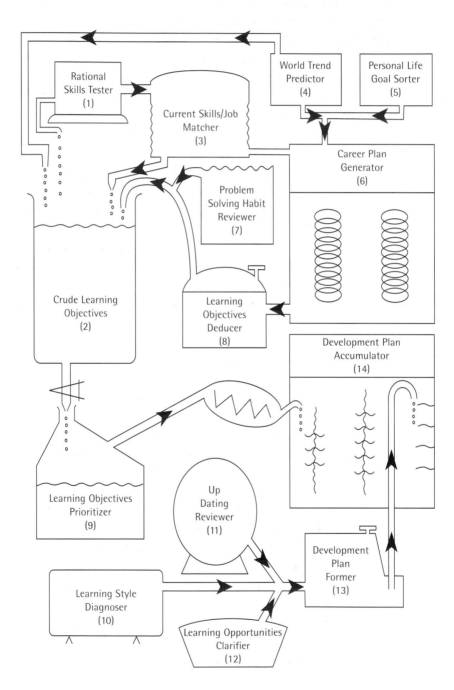

optimistic or pessimistic, conservative or imaginative, likely or unlikely. At this stage in the use of the workbook the user, in this application, is encouraged to discuss the career scenarios, and the thinking and assumptions going behind them with their managers, and to modify them in the light of any feedback. Care is taken to establish these plans as speculative, hopefully both realistic and imaginative, but certainly not definite. The aim of the workbook is to present the user with career scenarios that could be considered in the more formal career planning processes of the organization. The second part the workbook has a similar structure - a number of exercises that conclude with the Development Plan Accumulator (14). This is a short list of things that the person could usefully learn, with an accompanying learning plan for each one.

The second part starts with the Problem Solving Habit Reviewer (7) which invites the user to reflect on how they normally solve problems, and whether there are any new skills for doing so they could try to develop. The next step, the Learning Objectives Deducer (8), takes the user back to their career scenarios to consider what they could learn to enable them to follow those career patterns. Both of these activities add new ideas to the accumulating 'Crude Learning Objectives' list.

The exercises that then follow are concerned with what and how to learn. The Learning Objectives Prioritizer (9) takes the list of Crude Learning Objectives that has been accumulated and helps the user prioritize them. The user is encouraged particularly to think about whether they should emphasize getting better at what they are currently doing, or developing new skills for the future. Exercise 10 introduces the idea of learning style - that different people have different preferred ways of learning. Exercise 11 focuses on how the user normally keeps up to date with developments in their field. Exercise 12 is a mind-broadening exercise suggesting a wide range of formal and informal development opportunities surrounding us all. Exercise 13 uses these ideas to work out the 'hows' of the development plan.

As used in the Esso research laboratories the career scenarios and personal development plans formulated in this way were used as ideas to be followed up in the more formal appraisal, project planning and training systems of the organization. This resulted in more imaginative career options being envisaged and pursued. In at least one case a personal vision for a new kind of worked to a whole new project in the research and development strategy and the creation of that suggested job for the person - a clear example of the Level 5 process at work.

*

You could use this process to work out for yourself some career scenarios and a personal development plan. You could then use any opportunities that you find or create in your organization to discuss whether the career scenarios could become real, and whether you can pursue elements of the personal development plan with or without formal support.

Activity 11 starting on p.119 offers you a simplified framework within which to do this. If you use this exercise, or follow its logic, you will understand a process of forming and negotiating a career and self-development plan that takes into account where the organization is going and that even gives you a chance to influence it!

6 Working through Culture and the 'Psychological Contract'

It is important to understand an organization's culture from your development and career perspective. Culture is difficult to define and know because ways of seeing and doing things are taken for granted by an organization's members. It is said that we may not be aware of culture in the same way that fish may not be aware of water. But we do become aware of it when we visit or move somewhere else that operates with different and unfamiliar 'rules'. We are usually aware of culture when we first join an organization because it is something we have to accommodate to consciously as we learn to operate in the new environment.

Organizational cultures vary in many ways. Two sets of differences are most important from a career development point of view. Is your organization's culture either organization-centred (i.e. it plans for you) or, individual-centred (i.e. the responsibility for planning is yours)? Is your organization's culture either collaborative and supportive or, competitive and tough minded?

Another question is whether the culture is consistent in its development and career structuring, or gives a mixed message. For example, in practice the organization might say, in effect, 'You manage your development but we manage your career so you don't know what to prepare yourself for.' Alternatively, its position might be, 'We manage your development but it's up to you to find a career for yourself.'

Organizations also vary internally, having one culture in one part and a different one in another. Since your career may take you across some of the boundaries where cultures change, you can run into difficulties in managing your development and career unless you understand how the rules have changed and adapt your approach accordingly. For example, in many organizations there is a transition from 'rule following' to 'rule making' that comes somewhere in the journey from middle to senior management. Newly appointed senior managers may need to realize they have to negotiate further career moves informally, subtly and politically with their colleagues and the managing director, rather than wait for a formal system from the human resource department to allow them to put themselves forward - which may have been the process that initially got them where they are.

FOUR MANAGEMENT DEVELOPMENT PHILOSOPHIES

Organization-centred or person-centred

The most important manifestation of culture is the style of 'psychological contract' that applies to how you learn and develop, and how career changes happen. The most significant area of variation is between the 'organization-centred' psychological contract and the 'person-centred' psychological contract already mentioned.

The organization-centred contract is, at its extreme, the 'job for life in exchange for loyalty and obedience' deal. Here the employee is expected and expects to be placed in jobs and given training and development by those who plan careers, training and development on behalf of the organization.

The person-centred contract is, also at the extreme, where the manager/employee, as a temp, mercenary or hired hand, is employed for a specific job and regarded as responsible for their own career planning and development. The person is seen as a one man/woman business hiring out their skills to their current employer, or a portfolio of employers. They find their own work and keep their own skills up to date.

Most organizations work with a mixture of these philosophies - often with a basis in one or the other. The organization-centred approach will usually be moderated by a degree of consultation about job postings, the job-for-life principle overridden by redundancy programmes in periods of serious reorganization. Similarly the person-centred approach often encourages people to progress in an internal 'free' labour market with an insider's advantage, and with access to resources for learning at the person's initiative. While this distinction is useful, it has to be acknowledged that organizations vary over time between different sub-parts and for different career stages.

Tough or tender

Another dimension is 'tough' and 'tender'. The tough organizational contract subjugates the individual to the achievement of a perceived overarching goal: profitability, mission achievement, or the agenda of the most powerful individuals. The tender organization seeks to accommodate the employee's needs, wants, aspirations and aberrations as far as possible and within the bounds of running a viable organization. Consider the combination of these four dimensions shown in Figure 9 on p.66.

Now apply this to your working experience by marking the points on Activity 12 on p.134 representing the situation for each of your career periods identified in Activity 3.

ACTIVITY 12 Page 134

Fig 9: Different Philosophies of Corporate Career Management

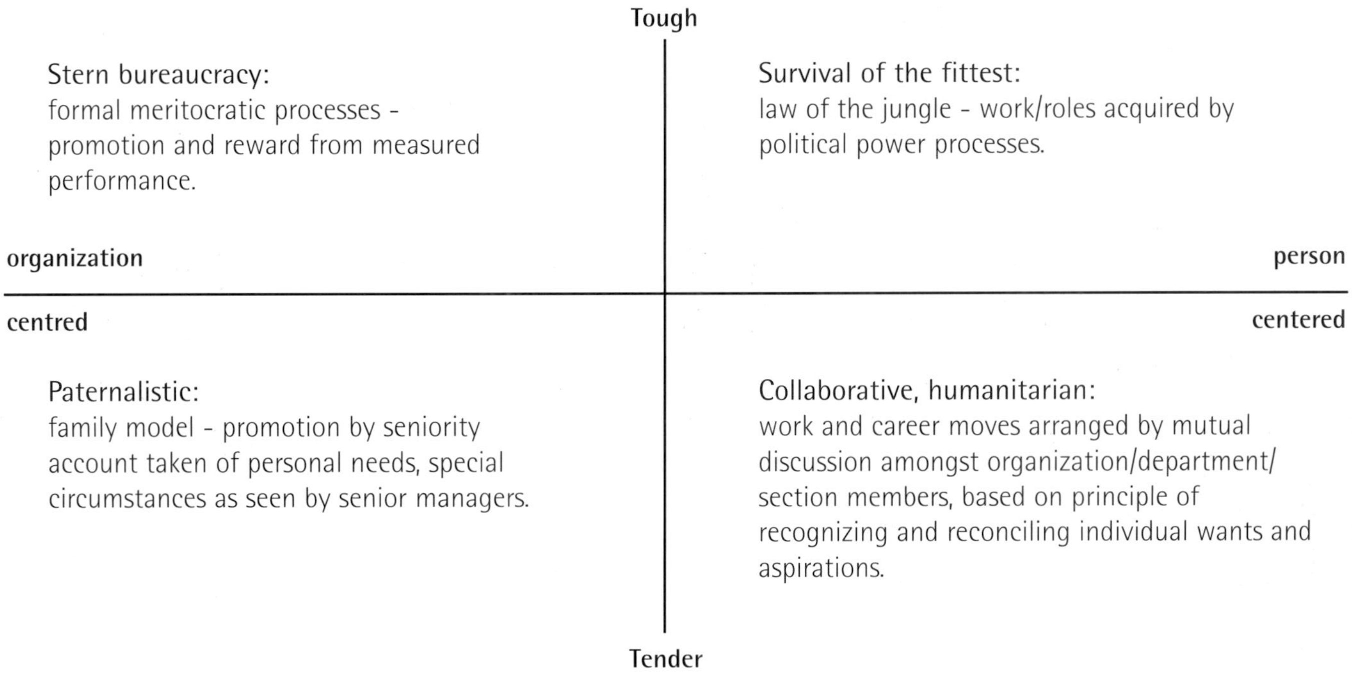

Tough

Stern bureaucracy:
formal meritocratic processes – promotion and reward from measured performance.

Survival of the fittest:
law of the jungle – work/roles acquired by political power processes.

organization centred ———————————————————— **person centered**

Paternalistic:
family model – promotion by seniority account taken of personal needs, special circumstances as seen by senior managers.

Collaborative, humanitarian:
work and career moves arranged by mutual discussion amongst organization/department/ section members, based on principle of recognizing and reconciling individual wants and aspirations.

Tender

It is possible to argue extensively about which philosophy is right, wrong, good, bad, enjoyable, distressing, efficient or inefficient. Yet all exist, and it would help you to reflect on the philosophies that you are most comfortable or agree with - and may have to deal with. In exploring this way of thinking about the career philosophy in different settings it may help to be aware that different parts of the same organization may work in different ways, and at the same time whole industrial or work sectors may have tendencies to one approach or another, because of the different traditions of their labour markets.

Activity 13 on p.135 helps you to evaluate your views on the different philosophies of corporate career management with which you may have to work.

FIVE ORGANIZATIONAL CULTURE TYPES

In thinking about organizational cultures, it helps to think of five types that contain different principles of custom and practice in relation to career moves and development processes.

Strict role culture

Basic procedures in the organization are designed to be meritocratic and fair within the framework of employment law and principles such as the equal opportunities legislation. Job descriptions, objective specification, performance measurement and appraisal and selection of people for jobs and promotions are highly systematized. Careers and career paths are planned, at least for those who are seen as key employees and for key jobs. There are formal training, education and development events on which employees are sent at specific career stages, or as an automatic process associated with moving into specific jobs or grades. In this culture training and development is strongly focused on a determined view of what the organization needs employees to know and be able to do.

Paternalistic role culture

This is similar to the above but with more of a tendency for people to get jobs based on seniority and turn taking; and for education, training and development to have a ritual element and to be partly focussed on what is thought to be good for people as a whole.

Task culture

Here, the organization is united by a strong belief in getting the job done in a technically and professionally effective way. People are more likely to be organized in project teams with different status roles and less of a hierarchy system. They are likely to be on different pay grades, reflecting the scarcity of their skills and level of development. Work is not so clearly clustered into job packages - people are expected to do what they can to contribute to the current work without worrying about tight job descriptions. Reputations are made through the project they have worked on and completed. Training and development tends to be technically and professionally focussed. Employees find and pursue learning opportunities on their own account but expect organizational support in terms of time and money when it can be justified through increase in their ability to perform important tasks. Employees in a task culture will be very aware of the development potential of work itself. They will actively seek work where they can use the latest technology and work with what they regard as leading edge problems, resources and procedures. Task cultures judge people by their portfolio of achievements. People in task cultures are seen, and see themselves, as belonging to the talent pool of the organization rather than a specific job.

- ## Person culture

The organization shows much care and concern for the well being of the individual in arranging careers and development. Work tends to be organized flexibly and informally. Decisions are made participatively amongst people who trust each other and share ambitions, wants, fears, feelings of competence and incompetence. Work and development is arranged to meet the needs of as many people as possible while still keeping the organization viable. The person culture may seem idealistic and unrealistic - and in formal work organizations it is almost certainly the rarest of the cultures. Nonetheless those who to operate in this way believe the approach leads to people working with enthusiasm, and with much less of the inefficiency that occurs in other approaches through misunderstandings, energy draining conflict and the failure to make full use of talent.

Power culture

This is one in which people look after themselves individually or in coalitions. The organization works largely on political principles. There is very little in the way of formal career planning and systems, and all is worked out by informal negotiation. The climate is competitive, with a general acceptance of the 'survival of the fittest' principle. Like the task culture, much learning occurs naturally as individuals discover what sources of power - money, resources, information, contacts - are useful and need to be acquired.

CONCLUSION

Figure 10 on p. 70 shows these cultures types superimposed on the management development philosophies grid shown in Figure 9. The organizational culture types are 'pure types' - like primary colours - and occasionally exist alone but are more often mixed in different proportions with others. Any particular culture is more likely to be a mixture. Also, different parts of organizations have

Fig 10: Corporate Career Management Philosophies as Organizational Cultures

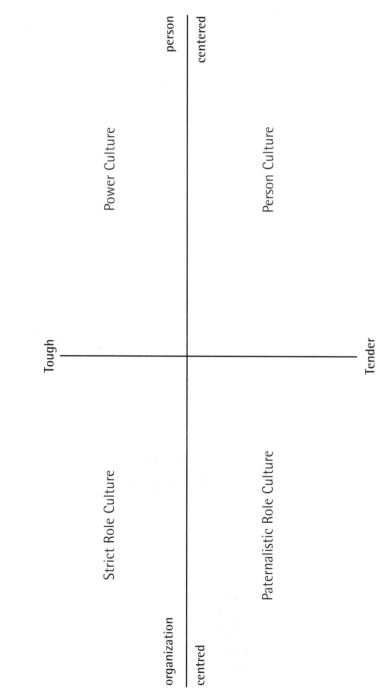

different cultures. There is no absolute common pattern for this but, in general, different parts have the cultures shown in the table below.

Organizational Part	Predominant Culture
Operations	Strict, paternalistic role or task culture
Research and development product/ service innovation/development	Task or person culture
Trouble shooting, fire fighting, reengineering, restructuring	Power or task culture
Strategic general management	Power culture

Figure 11 on p.72 shows these cultures diagrammatically.

Activity 14 on p.136 offers you some simple questions to think about the influence of culture on your career and development.

Fig 11: Organizational culture in different parts of an organization – general tendency

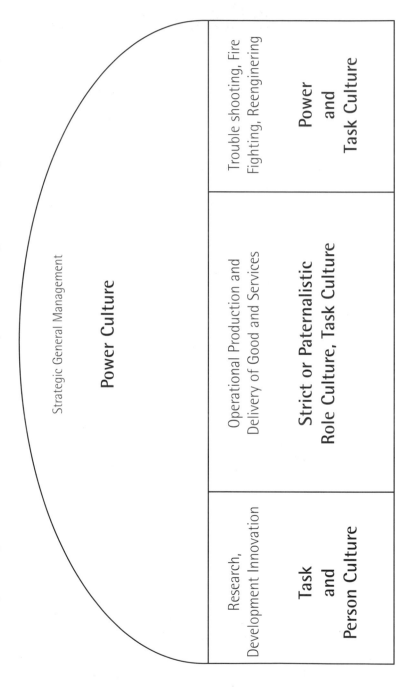

Strategic General Management

Power Culture

Research,
Development Innovation

**Task
and
Person Culture**

Operational Production and
Delivery of Good and Services

**Strict or Paternalistic
Role Culture, Task Culture**

Trouble shooting, Fire
Fighting, Reenginering

**Power
and
Task Culture**

7 Key Terms and Procedures in Management Development

Every specialism has its particular language, which is mostly inaccessible to the outsider. Management development is no exception although like other specialisms concerned with influencing and helping others it does and should make an effort to communicate in everyday language. However, some specialist language is arguably necessary and desirable since new ideas and practices need new labels. So just as general managers may be able to be more effective if they have a general understanding of the core language of accountancy, marketing and business strategy, so they could make better use of management development systems through understanding some of its core terms, concepts and practices.

This Chapter summarizes the core concepts, terms and practices of management development, and deals briefly with the ideas and issues and with how you might personally relate to them.

COMPETENCIES

Concept

Historically, the two sources of approach to helping people learn to manage have come from education and training. Education is about developing knowledge and understanding without necessarily the ability to do things, change things or make things happen; the ability to analyse problems without actually resolving them. Training has concentrated in contrast on how to do something, but without the corresponding mental activity of understanding that allows the trainee to modify action intelligently. Training is really more suitable for programmed activities rather than the unprogrammed essence of managerial work discussed in Chapter 1. The competency approach, involving the ability to act as well as to analyse unique situations, offers an attractive alternative.

Issues

There has been an understandable urge to make management development predictable and controllable - to show that it is a sensible investment. This has led to competency approaches being used in a rather mechanistic manner through attempts to define competencies in detail, and for whole organizations or parts of them to categorize learning events in terms of their competencies. This in effect turns management development back into training and assumes that managing is programmed rather than unprogrammed work. Such competency approaches, despite their considerable sophistication and complexity, never work for this very reason.

Competency approaches can also fall into the opposite trap, ironically the one that provided the rationale for their existence in the first place. Many competency initiatives are nothing but the endless writing of more and more detailed descriptions of actions and doing - theory not action. In other words they are the endless writing of menus and recipes without any cooking and eating - and yet the people involved cannot understand why they are still hungry. Confronted with this interpretation, management development specialists of this persuasion tend to respond by agreeing and then writing an action plan - another menu/recipe! They have actually lost touch with the concept of action and the ability to take it.

Personal implications

Beware of complex competency schemes that give you endless

lists and descriptions of things you should be doing, rather than encouragement to act intelligently and holistically and to learn from specific situations. Competencies and their language can be useful in helping you to envision new things you can learn, discussing with others what is involved in doing certain kinds of work and getting a general idea of what is offered by specific development programmes. But always remember that though menus and recipes are useful in planning and preparing, there has to be cooking and eating if the activity is to be useful - and only you can do that part.

EVALUATION

Concept

It is commonly accepted or believed that most or all projects and activities in management and organizational development are justified by their contribution to the achievement of a desired purpose. Learning, career structuring and strategic activities in management development are no exception to this. Whilst it is generally accepted that management development activities should be evaluated, in practice there is little done beyond collecting opinions on reaction-style questionnaires and feedback forms.

Issues

The problems with most thinking about evaluation are that it: (1) is entirely instrumental (2) takes a too narrowly unitarist view of purpose (3) is confused about causality (4) aspires to false objectivity and (5) is naïve about the true nature of development. We will look briefly at each of these criticisms in turn.

Evaluation has two aspects: deciding what you want (the valuing part) and working out if you are getting it (the instrumental part). If you contribute to managing an organization you set values and goals as well as achieve them. Whether it concerns a project meeting your aims, or helping some other project achieve its aims, evaluation should involve values negotiation as well as a judgment about goal achievement.

Organizations are best thought of as having multiple stakeholders and varying internal factions with different aspirations and interests. Any particular activity serves the purposes of different stakeholders and factions differentially, and evaluation involves clarifying and assessing of the achievement of these multiple goals.

Much evaluation thinking assumes that 'we' (the people evaluating 'our' project) are the clever part of the system and others are part of a predictable if complex machine through which we can achieve our purposes if we pull the right levers. This idea gets us into trouble. It is better to recognize that the 'system' out there is full of people and interest like ourselves, who are busy pursing their projects and purposes (and probably see us as part of the machinery through which they might do so). What happens and is achieved is much better seen as a consequence of the interactions of a whole set of actions taken in pursuit of a whole range of purposive agendas - which is not mechanically predictable.

It is difficult, some would say impossible, to achieve absolute objectivity about what matters most in management and organizations. Shared subjectivity - seeing if we can agree on our perceptions - is a better approach.

Finally, much evaluation thinking assumes you can know in advance what is to be achieved. True development is much more of a journey into unfamiliar territory, and while we may have a sense of a better way we may not know it in detail - at least until we see it. Evaluation approaches that insist on clarity of purpose before the event may actually inhibit or prevent development.

Personal implications

Organizations often give mixed and confused messages about evaluation. One minute they are treating you as 'customers' of their schemes, implying they are to be evaluated in terms of meeting your aims: the next they are evaluating you, or your behaviour, skills and values and so on to see if they fit in with their purpose.

There are two things to do from a personal point of view. The first is to have your own personal evaluation approach as part of managing the development of yourself and your career. This not only involves asking yourself how you will know if you have achieved what you aim to achieve - using this to reality-check your progress - but also being open to new possibilities and ideas. The second is to try to understand the organizational programmes around you and the purposes others have for them. Then you can work out how you do and want to fit in with them, align your purposes with theirs, and be aware of any conflicts of interest you may have to deal with.

PSYCHOMETRIC MEASUREMENT

Concept

Psychometric tests are widely used in organizations to 'measure' people for a variety of stated purposes: selection, placement, promoting self-understanding, diagnosing work 'problems', contributing to the identification of development needs, and so on. Indeed the construction, application, scoring, distribution and training uses of psychometrics is a major industry in itself.

The underlying idea is that the performance of organizations is made up of the performance of people, and that the performance of people is largely or entirely determined by their psychological characteristics - skills, attitudes, personality type, aptitudes, and so on. It seems to follow from this that the measurement of such personality characteristics is an essential part of managing human resources in business and organizations.

Psychometric instruments are almost entirely 'tick box' forms which ask you to answer questions - usually paper based but now occasionally computer presented. On completion, they are scored to produce 'measures' of your psychological characteristics.

The psychometric instruments regarded as 'proper' by the professional psychologists who work with them are generally supported by research, usually statistical. That is, they are primarily concerned with making sure the measures have two desirable qualities: validity (the extent to which they measure what they claim to measure) and reliability (the extent to which they do so consistently).

Issues

Despite their seeming 'scientific-ness' there are a number of critical points to be made about psychometrics as they are used in organizations. Firstly, they are rarely if ever used with the full procedures their apparent scientific rigour suggests. It is rare to find proof that any particular test has been tested for its ability to predict performance in the particular job for which it is used to select or reject you.

Secondly, and at their best, psychometrics only deal in probabilities. A good example is the notorious 11-plus examination in the UK, a largely psychometric intelligence-style test that was used to stream 11-year-olds into higher level academic education of 'secondary' education. Although more educationally able pupils on average were channelled towards more thorough academic education, and vice versa, thousands of pupils who would have benefited from higher quality education were prevented from getting it. And many that did get the opportunity were less able to benefit.

Thirdly, the underlying assumptions of the psychometric approach are questionable. The two main ones are that there are relatively stable (or absolutely stable) characteristics of the person that remain over time - from the time of testing over many years in employment; and that the way people behave and perform in work settings is strongly influenced or determined by these enduring characteristics. Anyone who has faith in their own ability to learn, and to be a sophisticated human being who can adapt their behaviour to different situations, will be rightly suspicious of mechanisms that shape their future on the assumption that they have a fixed personality type.

Fourthly, the way we work together to achieve things is arguably much more complex than the interaction of a set of fixed-personality robots. Much psychometric use encourages us to think of ourselves as machines, whereas we might in fact be better off thinking of ourselves as human beings with creativity, able to shape the way we are by choice and learning in different situations and in interaction with other people.

Having said that, psychometrics can be a rich source of ideas for how we think about ourselves, other people and our interactions with them. We need ideas to do this, and to explore what the future might be like and how we would like to shape it.

There have always been practices to help us think about these things, whether it was the words of the soothsayer, the entrails of chickens, tarot, astrology or many other well established and pre-modern methodologies that still survive today. In many ways psychometrics is in the same traditions presented in the currently (somewhat!) legitimate form of a scientific tool.

Whatever we think about the use of psychometrics in organizations, we need to recognise its status as a big industry. The catalogue of available tests resembles the phone book of a large city. There are thousands of professionals worldwide who devote their career to the development and application of psychometrics. The great majority of corporations of any size make substantial use of psychometrics in their personnel/employee relations/human resource procedures. Of all the things discussed in this book, it is perhaps the one most likely to impact on you - both in direct testing of yourself and the behind-the-scenes use of the data it generates.

Personal implications

Do not be overawed by psychometrics. The testers do not necessarily 'know' you better than you know yourself. You at least have the potential to be more flexible, adaptive, multi-faceted and self-determining than they may suggest. Any psychometric test offers you a way of thinking about some of the available strategies and tactics for the way you conduct yourself, and offers you an interpretation of your preferred or dominant strategies. Be very alert to the danger of, and resist where possible, arbitrary decisions being made about you on the basis of psychometric data.

At the risk of sounding unduly cynical, conspiracy-suspicious or even paranoid, the overstated scientific basis for psychometrics may be used to get you too uncritically accept portrayals of yourself that have important personal consequences. At worst, psychometrics may be misused to justify prejudicial, arbitrary or subjugating decisions.

The personnel/human resource world is at the start of an explosion in the use of information technology to 'data-warehouse' massive amounts of personal data. Almost anything that is assessed, measured or observed about you in an employment context will be stored in an analysable way to formulate all kinds of general policies and specific actions that will impinge on you. The 'image' of yourself presented in these massively enhanced data storage systems is becoming increasingly important. It is equally important that you manage and challenge this image.

PERSONNEL DEVELOPMENT PLANS

Concept

Many organizations suggest or insist that employees have personal development plans of the kind discussed in Chapter 4. They are created in a number of ways: as an output of appraisal processes, in the context of workshops or assessment centres, or through circulated paperwork systems. They all encourage you to formulate a plan for your own learning, dealing with what and how you might try to learn. They may encourage you to have action plans, milestones or deadlines to keep. They may or may not be followed up to see if you have been able to achieve them.

Personal development plans may be stand-alone processes, or linked to other mechanisms. Motorola, for example, has an explicit system of procedures in which employees are required to undertake an annual fixed number of training days. There is the 'Motorola University' catalogue of courses that employees are encouraged to use; training plans are logged and monitored; and completion of training day targets is directly assessed as a job requirement in annual appraisal.

Issues

Personal development plans, properly used, are a useful idea in developing yourself, your career and your organization. It is often argued that we put more effort into systematically planning the maintenance of our cars, houses, teeth or pensions than we do our own skills and abilities. Since it is the latter that allows us to earn the money to pay for the former, keeping our skills and abilities up to date is a good idea. However, personal development plans can go wrong, fall into disuse and get a bad name for a number of reasons:

1. They are better if they are linked to other processes, like career planning and implementation of new organizational strategies.

2. They are sometimes formulated but not followed through due to lack of encouragement and the provision of appropriate resources, including time, for their implementation.

3. They are sometimes forced on people in a way that feels over-controlling, manipulative, over-complicated, cumbersome and bureaucratic. They only work if they feel right and helpful to the people using them.

4. They can be insufficiently dynamic and insensitive to organizational and personal change. There is such a danger with personal development plans that assume you can

formulate a plan in one swift attempt and then implement it over a considerable length of time. All personal development plans should be seen as accessible to continuous revision, and have built-in mechanisms for this. For most of us, the context of our work is changing all the time, which throws up such continuing new challenges to learning. Also, the learning process itself creates new challenges - part of learning in any field is getting to know the further things we could learn. In any area that is genuinely new to us we 'do not know what we do not know'. As we enter a new field of understanding and ability we gain an increasingly detailed understanding of all the things there are to do and know. Our learning plans need to be continuously revised as we change through learning, and as the world changes around us.

Personal implications

It is worth having your own personal development plan whether or not it is encouraged by any organization you work for. The essentials for this plan are to have some idea about what it is useful for you to be learning right now, a view of how to do it, and then to be doing something about it.

Chapter 4 and Activity 11 offer a structure for you to formulate a personal development plan linked to other aspects of career and organizational development. However, it is better to have a simple plan, in terms of form and content, which you use rather than something complex that you do not. A plan that is not currently being pushed forward in any way is a sign of danger.

INVESTORS IN PEOPLE

Concept

Investors in People is a UK government sponsored scheme that assesses and certificates employing organizations against a good practice standard in the training and development of employees, and the systems surrounding this.

In terms of the model of corporate management development that is the core of this book, Investors in People is very much a Level 4 initiative that has explicit and demonstrable procedures to show that the training needs of all employees are considered and acted upon. It insists that all training and development is linked in a clear way to the implementation of extant and emerging organizational policies, plans, structures and procedures. Mechanisms must also be in place to ensure the implementation and monitoring of training.

The certification process involves inspection and audit, and is non-competitive - that is, organizations get the award if they meet the standards irrespective of how others perform. Organizations usually spend some time in preparing for the inspection/audit process, and in putting training systems and practices in place. Investors in People has a lot in common with various other quality-based corporate certification processes.

Issues

Investors in People is one, and probably the best, of the UK government backed initiatives to support training and development. Very many employees have sporadic and ad hoc training and development provisions (Levels 2 and 3 in the Ladder model). Implementing more generally applied training and development with a clear link to organizational purpose is the appropriate next step for many employers. There will be some organizations that have developed beyond what is required for Investors in People - approaching full learning organization functioning - for whom preparing for an Investors in People assessment would be non-developmental or even regressive. There may be some at the other end of the scale that need to introduce some form of rudimentary training and development, and a minimum cultural recognition of the usefulness of training and development before they adopt such systems.

As with all such initiatives there are some downsides and risks. All such schemes run the danger of becoming empty paperwork systems. Organizations may be tempted by the bureaucratic nature of the assessment process to develop paperwork schemes to give the appearance of compliance, or to adopt briefly the habits of 'best practice' in the period of assessment without their long-term continuation. Some organizations sign up to Investors in People at a senior level, while the operational commitment remains weak or tokenistic. Organizations within the sphere of UK government influence seem most likely to enroll. UK operating companies of large multi-nationals often feel, with some justification, that their own internal standards are as good or better, and do not feel the need for it or indeed in some cases appear not to have heard of it.

On achieving Investors in People status organizations need to think about the next steps. Levels 5 and 6 on the Ladder model - where training and development practice, and the associated career formation processes, contribute to the formulation of policy and strategy as well as its implementation - sustain interest and commitment towards creating learning companies or organizations. However, observers are suggesting that some organizations are not bothering to renew and maintain their 'Investors' status, raising questions about its enduring appeal and whether the downside of formal certification is a danger of valuing the badge over that which it is supposed to represent (see discussion of certification below).

Personal implications

If your employer has Investors in People status, or is pursing it, then in principle there should be some mechanisms in place, or being developed, to help you pursue training and development to increase your ability and value to the organization. If they are not clear to you, you could try to find out about them with a view to utilizing them.

Mission, vision and empowerment

Concept

A very high proportion of organizations today have 'mission' and 'vision' statements - they appear to have replaced the 'objectives' that were universal in previous decades. There is also much talk of 'empowerment' - giving people, or leaving with them, the power to use their own initiative and discretion in what they do.

The use of these terms, and the practices that go with them, are part of a broad trend in organizational and managerial philosophy or, more cynically, in the rhetoric and jargon of management. The general trend or aspiration can be described as the shift from external alignment of people to organizations, to reliance on a process of internal alignment.

Strategies of external alignment rely on objectives, job description, formal target setting for individuals and their measurement - possibly measuring and matching the competency requirements of the job to those of the person. This is 'external' because it relies on external job requirements, measurement, control, and providing incentives. To employees such processes have been unduly mechanistic, dehumanizing, and oppressive. To senior managers, such processes have created cumbersome organizations with expensive control systems that are difficult to change and make flexible.

The mission, vision or empowerment approach is based on internal alignment, and has proved popular and appealing, at first sight, for many parties to organizational life. In this philosophy employees (or members or partners as they tend to be called in this more 'inclusive' form of organization) behave in ways that align with organizational purpose not because they are externally constrained to do so, but because they believe in the rightfulness and usefulness of the organization's purpose, and are internally driven by these beliefs.

Individuals' beliefs may become aligned to an organization's purpose in a number of ways. Individuals may be drawn initially to particular organizations because of a belief in the value of what they do - they may have a vocational interest, a 'calling' for what they do. Secondly, people may be inspired by the leaders of an organization, who are seen as charismatic and worth following. Thirdly, people may participate in the forming of an organization's mission and come to support it both because of the outcome and process of this involvement. Fourthly, people may be persuaded to the values of an organization. There are different means of labelling this final process: by the neutral sociological term 'socialization' - the process by which we acquire the beliefs and values of our culture, society, professions, organizations; by the negative term 'brainwashing'; or by the positive term, 'bringing people on board'. The issue of the difference between 'brainwashing' and 'bringing people on board' is difficult and contentious. In our 'club' it is seen as 'bringing on board', in someone else's, it is 'brainwashing'. We can spot other organizations where people are organizational clones. We may be less aware of the values and behaviours that we have internalized.

Whatever may be the rights and wrongs of this, people are increasingly turning to work organizations not just as means through which to earn a living but as institutions that make life meaningful. It appears that in many ways work organizations are replacing religions, communities, extended families and nation-states as the sources of identity.

Issues

Although the mission, vision or empowerment movement is evident in many organizations, it is usually seen in conjunction with many of the systems of the external control model. Few organizations really operate in the way implied by the pure model. Only those organizations in the virtuous cycle of expansion and growth come nearest to it.

Most organizations are a mixture of internal and external control, and vary in the extent to which they have top-down, charismatic or indoctrinating missions versus a more participatory process. Organizations also vary in the extent to which the language of mission/vision/empowerment is cosmetic or genuinely translated into working practices. It is a reality of today's organizational world that many employees learn the art of appearing enthusiastic about missions and visions, and of talking the 'new language'. Yet it is difficult to know if this is done in a calculating manner or they are genuinely convinced. In many cases people come to believe in the mission of their organization as they become socialized. Equally, many employees spend long periods living a cynical double life. They pay lip service to the acceptable public language of the organization while being deeply cynical personally and in the company of trusted friends and colleagues. In today's complex world this is quite an understandable even necessary strategy.

Personal implications

It is well worth giving some thought to your own engagement with your organization. What is the balance of internal and external alignment between yourself and the organization? What is the congruence between your sense of purpose and the organization's? Which is shaping which? What is said in terms of the mission/vision/empowerment approach to your organization? How real is it in terms of practice and how it affects you? What is your own strategy for functioning in this context?

There are few or no right answers to these questions, but they should help you be aware of what is going on around you, to work out what you are comfortable with, and to have a strategy in which the two can co-exist.

ACTION LEARNING

Concept

Action Learning is a philosophy and method of learning. It has an interesting and complex history as a reaction to conventional management education, but can also be explained very simply. As the name implies, it is learning by doing in real situations. We all learn by discovery when we go about our work but we do not always make the best of the opportunity to do so. Action Learning and Action Learning Programmes help us do so by reflecting on our actions and making meaning from them. (For rich insight into the philosophy of the subject see the seminal text by the architect of Action Learning, Reg Revans, in his *ABC of Action Learning*, also published in this series).

The general idea is that we need to think about the problems and situations we face, be clear about the understanding that we have of them, act on the basis of this understanding, and modify it if necessary when we see the consequences of our action. The key is to work on real problems, and to see every action as a responsible and thought-through experiment.

Action Learning is usually done by joining a small group that meets periodically (called a 'set') helped by a facilitator (set adviser). Members usually take turns to describe the problems they are working on, examine their understandings of them, consider ideas from other members, commit themselves to action on the problem, report back and discuss the outcomes of previous actions taken.

Issues

Action Learning is very much a reaction and an alternative to expertise-based teaching, training and education. Many people find this attractive and appealing, as they sense that their problems do not have simple off-the-peg solutions. However, there is a danger of throwing the baby out with the bath water, and ignoring pre-existing solutions that can be useful. This is acknowledged in the theory of Action Learning, which suggests that pre-existing knowledge and method should be explored for solutions to problems before embarking on inventing your own.

As Action Learning is so closely involved in the individual's situation, the unquestioned assumptions in the culture surrounding that situation may limit the scope for action, unless something is done to help the learner stand back and question those assumptions. 'Critical Action Learning' is being suggested as a new direction that encourages learners to take a broader and more critical view of their work, thinking about ends as well as means.

Personal implications

Action Learning offers a very useful way of thinking about your learning and your engagement with work, whether or not you become involved in a formal Action Learning Programme. Your work is a learning experience and opportunity in itself, and once you have this idea learning becomes part of your work not an extra to it. For the reasons discussed, however, do not think you have to invent everything for yourself. See what others have invented, and remember that broader theoretical and educational ideas can be useful in getting a much broader perspective on what you are doing, and how you might break out of the prevailing and limiting mindsets of your work situation.

DIALOGUE

Concept

Dialogue can be called 'the talking cure for organizations'. It may sound facetious and simplistic to think that mere talk can solve organizational problems. Indeed in many situations too much talk - as opposed to taking action - may be seen as part of the problem rather than part of the solution.

However, it can be argued that organizations are made of knowledge and that this is the key and only asset of a business. Organizational knowledge is embedded in production processes and procedure - a car production line is an organizational memory or habit for making a motor car. Organizational knowledge exists in patents, copyrights, archives, records, the heads and minds of employees, and the organization's culture.

The organization prospers, or not, according to how well it coordinates the use of, and continuously keeps up to date, its knowledge in this broad sense. Dialogue is the key process by which this can be achieved. The word dialogue means something like 'the flow of meaning', and denotes the kind of talking that creates shared meaning. It is often contrasted with 'debate', which is the much more adversarial win/lose process of argument between individuals, groups or factions.

Issues

While the argument for dialogue is persuasive, the practice is more difficult. There is a contemporary fashion for 'dialogue events' in organizations, which attempt to get many people together for a fixed period, usually a day or two, to work with a structured discussion/problem solving agenda - often involving envisioning a strategic future and planning for its achievement. Such events may be useful, but probably only scratch the surface of the process described above.

It is better to think of dialogue as universal and continuous in organizations. All the communication, meetings, phone calls, e-mails and gossip are part of the continuous dialogue process. The question is how good is it, and what could make it better. (A masterly, practical account of organizational dialogue is given by Nancy M. Dixon in her book *Dialogue At Work*, also published in this series.)

Personal implications

Once you adopt the idea of dialogue you should be able to see how you are continuously part of it in any organization you work for, and how your own thinking connects and contributes to the collective thinking of the organization.

What kinds of organizational knowledge do you have access to and work with? What do you do to link it with other domains of organizational knowledge? Are you making a creative contribution to the collective view in your part of the organization?

EMPLOYABILITY

Concept

'Employability', much talked about in the human resource management or personnel profession, is determined by the skill and knowledge a person has, their attitude, and how they present themselves and come across in selection and recruitment processes.

Some organizations have staff with very specialist skills for which there is little demand elsewhere, and which can become obsolete as new technology develops - for example, IT staff with specialized skill in programming languages that fall out of use. From an organizational perspective, these people's employability is an issue as their careers are difficult to arrange. At the national level, the number of job vacancies and unemployment rate are attributed to a lack of employability.

Issues

Employability is usually thought of as a characteristic of the potential employee, but the employer's perception of employability is also an issue. Many employers take the view that prior experience in their specific sector or industry is necessary when it is not clear why this has to be so. Also, employability is region related - for example, there may be a national shortage of nurses, while at the same time there are nurses looking for work who are not able or cannot afford to move to the areas where nursing jobs exist. And for many walks of life, employability, for better or worse, is about your contacts, reputation, even favours owed, as much as 'objective' skills.

Personal implications

Think about your own employability - how easy it is for you to get a job or jobs in general, what skills and abilities you are selling, how good you are at the actual process of job seeking, and what contacts you have. Keep your curriculum vitae up to date and show it to other people for feedback. Think about any potential job move in terms of its impact - either way - on your employability. Finally, you may find courses or programmes available to you either inside or outside your current organization. In the UK, local training and enterprise councils are a likely source of information and help.

QUALIFICATIONS AND CERTIFICATION

Concept

There is an enormous range of academic, technical and professional qualifications that affect the world of work and employment. Some employers support staff in studying for various qualifications. Many people acquire qualifications on their own initiative through part-time study while in work, or during career breaks. Certain qualifications are mandatory in some jobs. In others they are regarded as desirable but not essential.

Employers generally take qualifications into account, though they are not the primary consideration in many employment decisions. Employers attach more importance to track record, and their own assessment and appraisal processes. There are even occasions where people are regarded as 'overqualified' for certain jobs - so that being qualified can be a disadvantage.

Issues

Generally, more and more people are obtaining qualifications and they are being taken increasingly seriously in employment decisions. This is perhaps because work is itself, becoming more expert as 'unskilled' work is automated, and as we all become 'knowledge workers'. Qualifications are also growing in importance because they seem to offer some kind of safeguard against risk - for the employee against the risk of not being employable, for the employer recruiting someone less able.

Yet there is something curious about qualifications, and how they work. While some, such as the qualifications to be an airline pilot, are directly related to the skills for the job and are regularly re-tested, there are others, like degrees taken decades ago (and this applies to the author!), where the 'graduate' would be unlikely to pass the exams today that led to the qualification. Nonetheless such qualifications count as evidence of a trained mind and commitment. But qualifications are not just about competence; there are also as the means by which people from certain social classes maintain preferential access to certain types of employment.

Personal implications

Whatever your views on the complex world of certification and qualification, it is something you need to think about and have a personal strategy towards your own career and development planning.

In addition to thinking about what qualifications, if any, are interesting, rewarding, or useful to pursue, and what this might do to the range of work available to you, you may also approach your employer regarding support for study. At the very least this means work time for study and fees and expenses for courses. Practice varies from meanness and discouragement to generous support in different organizations and for different people. Some employers encourage qualification-oriented study and provide in-company schemes as a means of locking in valuable employees. Some even make it a contractual formality to the extent of saying that employees have to pay back fees if they leave within a defined period after becoming qualified. It is worth seeing what kinds of 'deals', if any, are available to you and working out the advantages and disadvantages from your point of view.

*

These are only a sample of the more common concepts and practices in the diverse field of management development. You will be exposed to more, and more will emerge over time. In a discussion, always ask the meaning of a term you do not understand. Never pretend that you understand a term when you do not. Never allow your development or career to be significantly shaped by a mysterious, expert-owned word that you do not understand. All of these concepts/processes have a simple idea at their core. Each has strength and weaknesses. They all fit better in some situations than others and can be well or badly applied. They all provide you with opportunities if you understand them, or, if not, with the potential to be used against your interest. Quite often, specialists do not fully understand the terms, and they use them consciously or not, to develop their own mystique and to dissempower you. You need not allow this to happen.

8 Your Place in the Creation of Learning Companies or Organizations

The learning company or organization is the best available idea for enabling organizations to grow and develop as they wish, to optimize the satisfaction of all their stakeholders and to be fulfilling and rewarding places in which to work. Learning companies, as the term suggests, continuously learn to do these things collectively and better. The approach is the natural successor to total quality and business process re-engineering initiatives, which pursue efficiency largely through leanness - doing the same with less. Once this formula has reached its natural limits, a new formula is needed that seeks for development and growth. The learning organization is that formula. It is also the natural successor to UK government initiatives like Investors in People, either for those organizations that have gone beyond it, or become dissatisfied with it.

WHAT IS A LEARNING COMPANY?

In *The Learning Company: a strategy for sustainable development*, I and . my colleagues, Mike Pedler and Tom Boydell, formally defined a learning company as:

> 'an organization that facilitates the learning of all its
> members and consciously transforms itself and its
> context'.

When an organization functions at Level 5 or above in the Ladder Model presented in Chapter 1, the management development process helps to create a learning company by linking individual and organizational learning. If you as an individual can use the ideas in this book to make the organization behave at Levels 5 or 6 for you, then it is a contribution to the transformation of your organization into a learning company.

Here is the definition of the managerial role in the learning company:

> ⸱ 'The role of the manager is to learn on behalf of the organization and to help the organization implement that learning.'

If you see your role as continuously reviewing and updating your organization's practices and procedures and getting this accepted and implemented, you are creating the learning company process. The learning organization is an optimistic idea: it believes in a form or organization that is both socially and economically productive, and where satisfaction is increased for all stakeholders at once rather than through the trading off of one advantage against another.

The learning company philosophy does not claim that this is easy, nor does it wish to deny that the reality in many organizations is that people experience pain, stress, self-destruction, damage by seemingly insurmountable forces, frustration, waste, and so on. However, it does argue that there are better ways of carrying on in these difficult situations. At the extreme end of things, there are better ways of dealing with organizations or parts of them that need to be discontinued to release resources and space for new developments.

ADVANTAGES OF THE LEARNING COMPANY

There are three levels of functioning for an organization - generative, adaptive, and habitual - as set out in Figure 12 p.97.

At the minimal level of functioning - rare these days - organizations are habit driven and have a fixed set of routines. At the next level, organizations survive and prosper by continuous adaptation - continuously changing routines to keep up with the competitors, latest trends, changes in priorities, and changes in customer/client/consumer demands or tastes. At the third level, organizations create new processes and procedures that others have to adapt to - these are creative, leading organizations in their sectors or industries. These organizations do not merely respond to the demands of clients and customers but help them achieve new and desirable visions of what they could have in the future.

Fig 12: The Three Levels of Organizational Learning Functioning

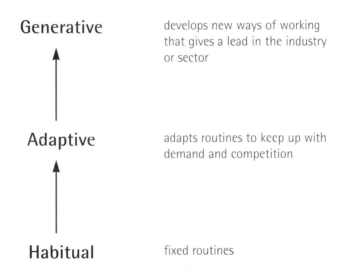

Generative   develops new ways of working that gives a lead in the industry or sector

Adaptive   adapts routines to keep up with demand and competition

Habitual   fixed routines

The model in Figure 12 also applies to you as an individual. To what extent do you operate on a long-standing set of habits? Do you have the ability to change and adapt to what goes on around you? Do you possess the practical creativity to do new things not previously envisioned? In general, organizations have or need a high proportion of people who operate at the same level as the organization as a whole. What does your work situation look like in these terms?

PROCESSES

Figure 13 below shows the core process by which organizations are believed to learn. All organizations have general policies, and broad aims and strategies for their achievement (they may be clearly stated or implicit). They are translated into action by operational plans (again formal and informal) which coordinate individuals' actions. People have ideas that they use both to shape their own particular action in their jobs defined by operational plans, and also to understand, debate and contribute to policy formation. Each of the figure-of-eights in this model (two vertical, two horizontal) represent the two-way processes connecting each of these activities. The two-way processes between them generate organizational learning.

Fig 13: The Core Learning Company Process

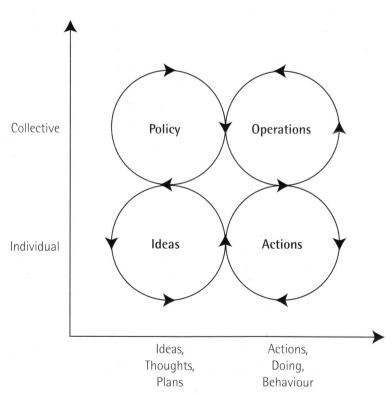

The ideas/action loop describes individual learning and the way you apply your ideas in your action. You should modify your ideas when you see the consequences of your action: the discovery loop in Figure 5. The action/operations loop in a learning company is also a two way process. The operational management plan is continuously modified in the light of the experiences of individuals putting it into practice. The policy/operations loop directs a learning company by formulating a policy and continuously modifying it in the light of the experience of putting it into operation. Lastly, the ideas/policy loop is the process by which all members of an organization participate in the process of creating and recreating policy - using, as discussed in Chapter 7, the process of dialogue.

This model describes the ideal of the learning company. Most real organizations diverge from this ideal and are less than optimally efficient at learning. Organizations diverge through being biased towards policy (all plans and no action); or operations (fixed habits); or actions (crisis management, chaos, muddling through); or ideas (all thinking and discussion, no agreement or action); or by being blocked if one or more of the 'flows' in Figure 13 is not working. Use this model to think about how your organization functions in terms of this model, about which parts of the process you are mainly involved in making work, and think about what different kinds of involvement you might want in the future.

PRACTICES

A learning organization has also been described in terms of eleven practices that activate the process described in Figure 13. Below is a summary of these practices or characteristics together with some of the things you can do to connect your personal learning with that of the organization you work in. A fuller treatment of the learning organization approach in practice is given in a companion book in this series: *A Concise Guide to the Learning Organization* by Mike Pedler and Kath Aspinwall.

Practice	Personal Opportunities
(1) *A learning approach to policies and strategies* are seen as continuous experiments.	(1) What is your role in applying policies and suggesting modifications in the light of this experience?
(2) *Participatory policy making:* policies are articulated and open to comment at all times. There is an acceptance that current policies are applied energetically - but can be criticized at the same time - and that this will influence the next policy formulation.	(2) Do you demand and make use of opportunities to be briefed on policies and strategies? Do you demand and make use of opportunities to comment on policies?
(3) *Informating:* Information technology is used to make the organization 'internally transparent'.	(3) Are you skilled in the use of whatever information technology is available to you at work? Do you use it to find out more about what is going on, and comment on it?
(4) *Formative accounting and control:* Budget, accounting and financial control systems give useful feedback on consequences of action, in a form that can be understood and used.	(4) Are you involved in the production or consumption of financial information? Do you demand that it is useful for monitoring anddecision making, and to help in understanding what is going on?
(5) *Internal exchange:* Different parts of an organization make arrangements with each other without tight, top-down control.	(5) Do you see the area where you work as an organization within an organization, and run it accordingly?

(6) *Reward flexibility:* Reward systems encourage learning and sensible experimentation in work, and the sharing of things learnt.	(6) Do you seek recognition for your learning, and willingness to share it with others, and do you encourage these things in anyone for whom you are responsible?
(7) *Enabling structures:* Structures are simple and flexible, are clear but capable of being changed?	(7) Do you demand clarity and change, simplicity in the structures that you work in?
(8) *Boundary workers as environmental scanners:* All those whose work gives them contact outside the organization use the opportunity to collect and pass intelligence about what is happening.	(8) Are you a boundary worker in these terms? Do you look out for useful information for your organization? Do you collect it and pass it on?
(9) *Inter-company learning:* learning companies learn from and with other organizations.	(9) Do you take an interest in what other organizations do, and try to draw lessons form this?
(10) *A learning climate:* the culture in a learning company is focused on problem solving and learning and encourages experiment.	(10) Do you take a 'solve and learn' rather than 'blame and punish' attitude when things go wrong? Do you support experimentation for yourself and others?
(11) *Self-development opportunities for all:* Members of learning companies are encouraged to develop themselves, and given resources and support to do so.	(11) Do you demand, find out about, and use opportunities and resources for your development? Do you encourage and support this for others?

CONCLUSION

The practical purpose of this book has been to empower you, as an acting or potential manager, to develop yourself, your career, and with this your organization, in a way that fits the learning company vision. If you are a colleague in the world of management development work, I hope you can use these ideas to join me in enabling managers to take this step. I hope we can all progress with these ideas in the spirit of learning - trying them out and developing the ideas in the light of the experience of doing so.

Activities

Activity 1: Corporate management development effectiveness level

Tick the levels and describe the circumstances

(6) As (5) plus new policies are implemented as learning experiments, and I feel part of this.

(5) As (4) plus I can see how my skills and visions, and those of my colleagues, influence the policies we are implementing.

(4) I pursue learning opportunities to support career plans that fit in with what is known and planned about the future of the organization.

(3) I have learning opportunities and career discussions that fit together and influence each other, but it is not clear how they relate to changes in organizational direction.

(2) Specific, isolated learning or career development events do occasionally impact on me, but are disconnected from anything else.

(1) All learning and career development is left to chance, but the informal processes allow me to have some influence over my future and to prepare myself for it.

(0) I am unable to form any view of the future of my work, or to prepare for the future either through formal or informal processes.

From John Burgoyne (1999) *Developing Yourself, Your Career and Your Organization*, Lemos & Crane, London

Your current situation		The best you remember		The worst you remember	
Rate	describe	Rate	describe	Rate	describe

From John Burgoyne (1999) *Developing Yourself, Your Career and Your Organization*, Lemos & Crane, London

Activity 2: What is a manager? Are you one?

(1) Is the word 'manager' in your title?　　yes ☐　no ☐

(2) Is your job described in any other way
that implies 'organizing the organization'
administrator, director, coordinator ... ?　yes ☐　no ☐

(3) Do people formally report to you?　　yes ☐　no ☐

(4) Do you have discretion to allocate
resources to different uses?　　yes ☐　no ☐

(5) Are you primarily concerned with getting
things done through other people?　yes ☐　no ☐

(6) Do you make decisions and take actions
that have a broad impact across your
organization?　　yes ☐　no ☐

(7) Do you primarily work on problems and
issues for which there are no off-the-shelf,
technical or professional solutions?　yes ☐　no ☐

From John Burgoyne (1999) *Developing Yourself, Your Career and Your Organization,*
Lemos & Crane, London

Each of the above questions implies a different criterion for what counts as 'managing' or being a 'manager'. In general, there are no rights or wrongs. However, for the purpose of this book, it is largely the last of these that matters - dealing with uncertainty, or non-routine problems and issues. This is the defining feature that makes education, training, learning and career formation different for managers compared with other occupations.

Most of the other criteria imply this 'uncertainty' element : people are unpredictable so managing them is uncertain; allocating resources often implies judgment rather than calculation; the big and influential decisions are the unclear but influential ones, and so on.

From John Burgoyne (1999) *Developing Yourself, Your Career and Your Organization*, Lemos & Crane, London

Activity 3: Your career

Remind yourself of your 'career' to date. Put down your 'career steps' and dates as you would on an application form or curriculum vitae.

These may be formal employment posts or if you are at an earlier stage in your life/career this may include educational/training periods, or indeed anything that makes sense to you of what you have been doing in your work autobiography.

This record will be used as a basis for subsequent Activities. Use more sheets if necessary

Career step	Dates

From John Burgoyne (1999) *Developing Yourself, Your Career and Your Organization*, Lemos & Crane, London

Activity 4: Career steps as deals and negotiations

Reflect on the process by which you found yourself at each of your 'career steps' (as described in Activity 3). Think about the following questions and make some notes on a separate sheet about what happened and what insights you gained from these events. Look at as many of your career steps as you like. If you have many of them, concentrate on those that seem most interesting or had the most impact on your life.

Transition to career steps: Question	Number:	Number:	Number:
(1) Did you choose your career step, did it choose you, or was it negotiated?	☐	☐	☐
(2) Was the choice based on an accurate prior exchange of information? Did any surprises later emerge due to lack of exchange of prior information?	☐	☐	☐
(3) As a deal, did you make the best use of your opportunity? Were there aspects of what was agreed that were later regretted on either side?	☐	☐	☐
(4) Was the deal clear enough? Did misunderstandings later emerge?	☐	☐	☐

From John Burgoyne (1999) *Developing Yourself, Your Career and Your Organization*, Lemos & Crane, London

Activity 5: Your experience of 'developmental' and 'structural' tactics

Developmental Tactics	Do these happen in your organization?	Have you experienced these?
Courses	yes ☐ no ☐	yes ☐ no ☐
Mentoring	yes ☐ no ☐	yes ☐ no ☐
Coaching	yes ☐ no ☐	yes ☐ no ☐
Open and distance learning	yes ☐ no ☐	yes ☐ no ☐
Actual and virtual learning resource centres	yes ☐ no ☐	yes ☐ no ☐
Action Learning	yes ☐ no ☐	yes ☐ no ☐
Self development and self managed learning	yes ☐ no ☐	yes ☐ no ☐
Shadowing	yes ☐ no ☐	yes ☐ no ☐
Attachments and secondments	yes ☐ no ☐	yes ☐ no ☐

From John Burgoyne (1999) *Developing Yourself, Your Career and Your Organization*, Lemos & Crane, London

Developmental Tactics	Do these happen in your organization?		Have you experienced these?	
Floor coaching	yes ☐	no ☐	yes ☐	no ☐
Case studies	yes ☐	no ☐	yes ☐	no ☐
Organizational visits	yes ☐	no ☐	yes ☐	no ☐
Simulations, business games and role playing	yes ☐	no ☐	yes ☐	no ☐

Structural Tactics

	Do these happen in your organization?		Have you experienced these?	
Succession planning	yes ☐	no ☐	yes ☐	no ☐
Fast track schemes	yes ☐	no ☐	yes ☐	no ☐
Assessment centres	yes ☐	no ☐	yes ☐	no ☐
Psychometric measurement	yes ☐	no ☐	yes ☐	no ☐
Person by person competency databases	yes ☐	no ☐	yes ☐	no ☐
Head hunting – internal and external	yes ☐	no ☐	yes ☐	no ☐

From John Burgoyne (1999) *Developing Yourself, Your Career and Your Organization*, Lemos & Crane, London

Structural Tactics	Do these happen in your organization?	Have you experienced these?
Open and semi-open internal labour marketplaces	yes ☐ no ☐	yes ☐ no ☐
Shadowing	yes ☐ no ☐	yes ☐ no ☐
Attachments and secondments	yes ☐ no ☐	yes ☐ no ☐

Reflecting on your experiences with these 'tactics', and thinking back to Activity 1:

Do the 'structural' and 'developmental' fit and support each other?   yes ☐ no ☐

Can you see a link to the policy/strategy of the organization?   yes ☐ no ☐

From John Burgoyne (1999) *Developing Yourself, Your Career and Your Organization*, Lemos & Crane, London

Activity 6: Exploring the structural and developmental facets of your career

Significant career step

What did you do?

What did you study?

What did you learn in this period?

How have you used this - at the time or later?

From John Burgoyne (1999) *Developing Yourself, Your Career and Your Organization,* Lemos & Crane, London

Activity 7: Exploring your 'natural' learning

(1) Think of something that you have done where you were effective in your action. Give it a name and write a few sentences on what you did.

(2) What would you say were the main skills, abilities or other attributes that enabled you to do this?

(3) How did you acquire these and from what source? (If you have difficulty with this recall the earliest you had it, and the latest

(4) Count, estimate or guess the proportion of useful learning from Natural and Contrived acquired learning

NATURAL   CONTRIVED

%   %

From John Burgoyne (1999) *Developing Yourself, Your Career and Your Organization*, Lemos & Crane, London

Activity 8: Linking learning and career development help

If 'structural' and 'developmental' tactics that impinge on you are linked you should be able to see the connections. Check this by seeing how easily you can answer the following two sets of questions. The first set starts from any 'learning' event you have the been involved in. The second set from any 'structural' event (annual appraisals, assessment centres, career potential reviews).

1. Learning event	

What should you have learnt from it?	

What should you have been able to do as a result?	

What career scenario did this support for you?	

What career scenario did this support that suited your employer?	

From John Burgoyne (1999) *Developing Yourself, Your Career and Your Organization*, Lemos & Crane, London

```
┌─────────────────────────┐      ╭──────────────╮
│ 2. Performance or career│      │              │
│ development review process│    │              │
└─────────────────────────┘      ╰──────────────╯
            │
            ▼
┌─────────────────────────┐      ╭──────────────╮
│    What learning goals  │      │              │
│     were identified?    │      │              │
└─────────────────────────┘      ╰──────────────╯
            │
            ▼
┌─────────────────────────┐      ╭──────────────╮
│ What follow up was planned? │  │              │
└─────────────────────────┘      ╰──────────────╯
            │
            ▼
┌─────────────────────────┐      ╭──────────────╮
│   How did it assume you │      │              │
│      would learn?       │      │              │
└─────────────────────────┘      ╰──────────────╯
```

From John Burgoyne (1999) *Developing Yourself, Your Career and Your Organization*, Lemos & Crane, London

Activity 9: The management development specialists

(1) Who are the 'management development' specialists in your world (by name and title)

(2) What services, systems do they run or offer?

(3) What use can you make of them?

ACTIVITY 10: Your learning history

Step 1: Draw a line in the 'graph' below showing how much or how little you remember learning at different stages in your work life. Work with your own idea of what learning means, but bear in mind the working definition of 'getting clearer about what you should do, and better at doing it'. Remember, however, that feeling incompetent or being unclear is often a stage in the learning process.

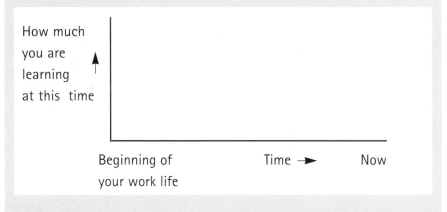

How much you are learning at this time

Beginning of your work life   Time ➝   Now

Step 2: Consider the peaks and troughs of your graph, and see what conclusions you can draw about (a) and (b) below.

(a) *How* you learn best

(b) In what *circumstances* you learn best

From John Burgoyne (1999) *Developing Yourself, Your Career and Your Organization*, Lemos & Crane, London

Activity 11: A personal career and development plan

To form a personal career and development plan, complete the nine separate exercises that follow (Activity 11.1 to Activity 11.9)
By the end of this Activity you should have an outline personal development plan that is:

- *thought through in the context of some career scenarios that you might follow*

- *reflective of how you learn best and the opportunities that you have*

- *likely to be simple for you to start to implement*

- *useful as a basis for talking to anyone in any organization you work for whose job it is to help with your education, training and development. If you know of people who can help you refine and implement your plan then approach them.*

From John Burgoyne (1999) *Developing Yourself, Your Career and Your Organization*, Lemos & Crane, London

Activity 11.1: Personal career and development plan: Skills and abilities

Note your skills and abilities under the three headings below.

(A) Abilities that I have but do not use in my current work:

(B) Abilities that I have and do use in my current work:

(C) Abilities that I do not have which would be useful in my current work:

From John Burgoyne (1999) *Developing Yourself, Your Career and Your Organization,* Lemos & Crane, London

ACTIVITY 11.2: Personal career and development plan: Learning objectives

Copy below your list from box (C) in Activity 11.1 (Abilities that I do not have which would be useful in my current work)

Possible personal learning objectives:

From John Burgoyne (1999) *Developing Yourself, Your Career and Your Organization,* Lemos & Crane, London

ACTIVITY 11.3: Personal career and development plan: Trends affecting my work

Make notes in boxes (A) to (E) of any changes you feel are affecting your work or organization, or will do so in the future. Write some words or phrases to describe how your world of work is likely to be different from the present in, say, five to ten years' time.

(A) Technical

(B) Social

(C) Economic

(D) Political

(E) Market

Next, having thought about trends and the future, consider whether there are things that you should or would like to learn. This could be anything from more general awareness of trends to the development of specific skills that might become more critical in the future. Add these to the list of possible personal learning objectives in Activity 11.2.

From John Burgoyne (1999) *Developing Yourself, Your Career and Your Organization*, Lemos & Crane, London

ACTIVITY 11.4: Personal career and development plan: Life goals, opportunities and constraints

Make notes on what you now get or would like to get, personally, out of work. (Here are a few possibilities: wealth, power, freedom, utilization of abilities, respect, satisfying relationships with others, leadership, prestige, status, autonomy, self-expression, fame.)

Next, reflect on how your 'life goals' are different now from how they were in the past, and consider how they might change in the future. What will be your goals and priorities in five years' time?

 From John Burgoyne (1999) *Developing Yourself, Your Career and Your Organization*, Lemos & Crane, London

Next, make a note of any constraints and opportunities you may have (e.g. place of work, availability to travel) arising from the social, domestic, physical aspects of your life, and note any changes that are likely to occur in the next five years.

Next, consider the points you have made in this Activity and work out if there are any areas of skill, understanding and ability that would help you pursue your goals. Add them to the list you have compiled in Activity 11.2.

From John Burgoyne (1999) *Developing Yourself, Your Career and Your Organization,* Lemos & Crane, London

ACTIVITY 11.5: A personal career and development plan: career scenarios

Use this Activity to sketch out three different career visions of your future. In doing this you should take into account all the issues you have reviewed so far - your abilities, your aims in life, your constraints and opportunities, your vision of the future. You should choose a timescale appropriate for yourself - it may be one year or two, it may be decades. You may wish to visualize just one job/role/activity change or a whole sequence. You could use the three scenarios to explore three possible futures that are different or you might find it useful to think in terms of 'normal', 'optimistic' and 'pessimistic' ones. You may be able to discuss the scenarios with friends and colleagues to get their view on how realistic they are, or you may be able to use them in appraisal or other kinds of formal meeting to 'ask' if any of them can become reality. Consider asking your boss or someone in personnel/human resources whether it is realistic to expect such a career, and what it takes to make that happen.

After you have completed this Activity, think about the career scenarios in terms of your ability to do things you would like, or might have liked to do. Add to your list in Activity 11-2 any learning needs that arise.

From John Burgoyne (1999) *Developing Yourself, Your Career and Your Organization*, Lemos & Crane, London

A

Career Scenario 1

Career Scenario 2

Career Scenario 3

From John Burgoyne (1999) *Developing Yourself, Your Career and Your Organization*, Lemos & Crane, London

Activity 11.6: Personal career and development plan: Prioritizing learning objectives

Copy out the learning objectives you have listed in Activity 11.2, combining any that are more or less the same.

The next step is to prioritize these learning goals. Choose no more than six. The priorities may be obvious to you but, if not, think which ones would make the biggest difference to you. Consider the balance between the short-term and long-term benefits of your learning goals. Short-term ones will help you with what you are doing now; long-term ones are for some of the things you envisage doing in the future.

Summarize possible current learning goals, say up to 6, based on what you have written in Activity 11.2. Put together those that are the same or similar.

Prioritize these goals - 1 to 6 - in order of importance

From John Burgoyne (1999) *Developing Yourself, Your Career and Your Organization*, Lemos & Crane, London

Activity 11.7: Your personal career and development plan

Write your priority learning goals (up to six of them) on the left-hand column, evenly spaced down the page. The complete the right-hand column so that you have a personal development plan. The next steps in Activities 11.8 and 11.9 help you to take a broad view of the options for this, and to consider what kinds of learning processes help you best.

What are you going to
set out to learn?

How are you
going to learn it?

From John Burgoyne (1999) *Developing Yourself, Your Career and Your Organization*, Lemos & Crane, London

Activity 11.8: Personal career and development plan: How do you learn best?

Use this Activity to make notes about how you learn best. Think about times, episodes, events when you have learnt a lot, or not very much. Think about formal learning events and also about work and life events - experiences and incidents from which you have learnt. Think about people, ideas, issues, places, organizations that have helped you to learn.

- What or who helps you to learn?
- What is the process? (being told, shown, trying it out, watching, thinking, etc)
- What are the circumstances in which you learn most?
- What resources and what forms of assistance help you most?

From John Burgoyne (1999) *Developing Yourself, Your Career and Your Organization,* Lemos & Crane, London

From John Burgoyne (1999) *Developing Yourself, Your Career and Your Organization*, Lemos & Crane, London

ACTIVITY 11.9: Personal career and development plan: Formal and informal learning opportunities

List all the possible learning opportunities that are available to you. This can include formal study on long courses but also very simple things like talking to a colleague, reading an article, phoning round contacts and acquaintances and experimenting with a different way of doing something. Think of the resources for learning available from your employer and also in the community - local colleges, libraries, adult education facilities and part-time study opportunities. Be as imaginative as possible. Some of the most useful ideas may be simple, small in scale and easy and cheap to pursue.

Your creative list of all the learning opportunities that are available to you:

From John Burgoyne (1999) *Developing Yourself, Your Career and Your Organization,* Lemos & Crane, London

Now complete your personal career and development plan in Activity 11.7 using the ideas you reviewed in Activities 11.8 and 11.9.

From John Burgoyne (1999) *Developing Yourself, Your Career and Your Organization,* Lemos & Crane, London

Activity 12: Different philosophies of corporate career management

Draw a line marked with dates locating the different periods of your career so far.

Tough

Stern Bureaucracy   Survival of the fittest

organization   person

centred   centred

Paternalistic   Collaborative, humanitarian

Tender

From John Burgoyne (1999) *Developing Yourself, Your Career and Your Organization*, Lemos & Crane, London

Activity 13: Different philosophies of corporate career management

Mark (a) to (d) areas that: (a) you (would) like to work in; (b) you feel skilled in coping with; (c) you feel is morally and ethically acceptable; (d) you may have to work in to achieve your career aspirations.

Tough

Stern Bureaucracy   Survival of the fittest

organization   person

centred   centred

Paternalistic   Collaborative, humanitarian

Tender

From John Burgoyne (1999) *Developing Yourself, Your Career and Your Organization,* Lemos & Crane, London

Activity 14: Culture and your career

(1) Look back at your answers to Activity 3 and consider what were the predominant cultures in your different career steps? Label them:

SRC	strict role culture
PRC	paternalistic role culture
TC	task culture
PrsC	person culture
PwrC	power culture

(2) Look again at Figure 11 (on p.72) and think generally about the kind of work that you would like to do in the future. What might be the predominant culture in which you would find such work?

(3) How is this future different from what you have been used to?

(4) What are the implications for how you need to pursue your career and development from now on?

From John Burgoyne (1999) *Developing Yourself, Your Career and Your Organization*, Lemos & Crane, London

Bibliography and suggested reading

Burgoyne J.G. (1995) 'Learning from experience: from individual discovery to meta-dialogue via the evolution of transitional myths', *Personnel Review 24* (6) pp62-73.

Burgoyne J. G. and Germain C. (1984) 'Self development and career planning: an exercise in mutual benefit'. *Personnel Management.* April. pp21-23. (Modifies ideas formulated by Charles Handy, in turn based on the ideas of Roger Harrison)

De Geus A. P. (1988) 'Planning as Learning', *Harvard Business Review.* March/April. 66 (2) pp70-74.

Dixon N. M. (1998) *Dialogue At Work* Lemos & Crane, London.

Fayol H. (1949) *General and Industrial Management* Pitman, London.

Fox S. and McLeay S. (1992) 'An approach to researching managerial labour markets : HRM, corporate strategy and financial performance in UK manufacturing'. *International Journal of Human Resource Management.* (3) pp523 - 554.

Fox S., McLeay S., Tanton M. ,Burgoyne J. and Easterby-Smith M. (1990) 'Managerial Labour Markets: Human Resource Management and Corporate Performance'. *ESRC Project Final Report.*

Handy C.B. (1985) *Understanding Organizations.* 3rd. edn Penguin, Harmondsworth.

Harrison R. (1995) *The Collected Papers of Roger Harrison*. McGraw-Hill, Maidenhead.

McLaughlin M. and Thorpe R. (1993) 'Action Learning - a paradigm in emergence: the problems facing a challenge to traditional management education and development.' *British Journal of Management*. 14 pp19-27.

Pedler M.J. (1997) 'Action Learning', in Burgoyne J.G. and Reynolds M. (eds.) *Management Learning: Integrating Perspectives on Theory and Practice*. Sage, London.

Pedler M. J. and Aspinwall K. (1998) *A Concise Guide to the Learning Organization*. Lemos & Crane, London.

Pedler M.J., Burgoyne J.G. and Boydell T.H. (1996) *The Learning Company: A Strategy for Sustainable Development* 2nd Ed. McGraw Hill, Maidenhead.

Prahalad C.K. and Hamel G. (1990) "The Core Competence of the Corporation" *Harvard Business Review*. 68 (3) pp79-91.

Revans R. W. (1998) *ABC of Action Learning*. Lemos & Crane, London.

Schein E. (1978) Career Dynamics: *Matching Individual and Organizational Needs*. Addison Wesley, Reading.

Simon H. A. (1957) *Administrative Behaviour*. 2nd ed. Macmillan, New York.

Taylor F. W. (1967) (orig. 1911) *The Principles of Scientific Management*. W. W. Norton, New York.

Rix A. Parkinson R. and Gaunt R. (1993) 'Investors in People: A qualitative study of employers'. *Employment Department Research Series* No. 21.

Willmott H. (1997) 'Critical Management Learning' In: Burgoyne J.G. and Reynolds M. (eds.) *Management Learning: Integrating Perspectives on Theory and Practice*. Sage, London.

Index

Also published in the Mike Pedler Library

Managing Yourself

Over 40,000 copies sold.

This new edition of Mike Pedler and Tom Boydell's best-selling guide develops your ability as a manager to become proactive rather than controlled by events and other people. Including a workbook of activities *Managing Yourself* develops and sustains your:

- skills - social and technical
- action - getting things done
- health - physical, mental and emotional
- identity - valuing and being yourself.

Tried and tested, and as relevant now as when first published in the 1980s, this book's practical philosophy that leads to improved management of self and others will find new converts in organizations from all sectors.

About the Authors

Dr Mike Pedler is the series editor of the Mike Pedler Library, his other books in this series include *A Concise Guide to the Learning Organization.* **Dr Tom Boydell** is a writer and consultant who has worked with clients throughout the world, including the European Commission and the ILO. Along with Mike Pedler and John Burgoyne, he is the co-founder of the Learning Company Project.

ISBN 1-898001-55-3

Also published in the Mike Pedler Library

ABC of Action Learning

Professor Reg Revans' distils the lessons of decades of experience applying the theory he originated – Action Learning. In today's rapidly changing environment where learning is a necessary prerequisite to innovation, Revans' ideas are crucial in empowering the individual manager or leader to act and to learn from action. **ABC of Action Learning** gives you:

- structures to implement Action Learning programmes based on an understanding of its operational forms
- insights gained from experiences of launching Action Learning world-wide
- conditions for bringing about learning in the organization as a whole system.

"One of the most profound management thinkers Britain has produced."

The Observer.

"Interest in Revans' ideas pours in from around the world"

Financial Times.

"Revans is the management genius of this country - the thinker we should be drawing on."

Dr Ronnie Lessen, City Business School.

"Revans is one of the great originals."

Sir Peter Parker, London School of Economics.

About the Author

Professor Reg Revans is one of the UK's original business thinkers. Appointed as Britain's first professor of industrial administration in the 1960s, Reg Revans has worked with managers in Britain, Europe, Africa, North America and India. In 1998 he was made a Freeman of the City of London.

ISBN 1-898001-42-1

Also published in the Mike Pedler Library

Dialogue at Work

Seventy-five per cent of a manager's day is spent in conversation. Much practised but imperfectly understood, **Professor Dixon** outlines the nature of talk and how it can be developed into 'dialogue' – increasingly seen as an essential tool in managing knowledge and change. ***Dialogue at Work*** gives you:

- an understanding of the relationship between talk and development in organizations; how dialogue differs from the skilled talk that goes on all the time
- the ability to recognise talk that hinders development and means of rectifying this on an individual and group basis
- practical ideas based on research with leading companies
- outlines of the leading theories on the nature and function of dialogue.

"Nancy Dixon's work has contributed a great deal to the development of our Executives at Unisys."

Amelia Hakim, Unisys.

"Extremely useful in my consulting practice."

Ellen Glanz, Glanz Associates, USA.

About the Author

Professor Nancy M Dixon is Associate Professor of Administrative Sciences at the George Washington University. She has served as a consultant to numerous companies including Unisys, IBM, FAA and is the acclaimed author of *The Organizational Learning Cycle*.

ISBN 1-898001-41-3

A Concise Guide to the Learning Organization

Managing change and learning is the No.1 task - wherever you work. *A Concise Guide to the Learning Organization* enables you, as a leader or manager, facing unprecedented and unpredictable change to utilise practical principles and models that will enhance your organization's capacity to learn. This accessible guide includes activities and gives you:

- a practical understanding of the nature of organizational learning
- ideas for future development - how learning organizations can contribute to the wider environment and their role in creating the Good Society
- case studies that give insight into how organizations have enhanced their own learning.

"I found the book full of wise insights, thought-provoking questions and starkly put dilemmas."

David Megginson, Sheffield Business School.

About the Author

Dr Mike Pedler, series editor of the Mike Pedler Library, is co-author of *Managing Yourself* and many other publications. **Kath Aspinwall** holds senior lecturer positions at Sheffield Hallam University and at the University of York. She is the co-author of *Perfect plc?* and author of *Leading the Learning School*.

ISBN 1-898001-43-X

Also published in the Mike Pedler Library

Resolving Conflicts in Organizations

Conflicts are common in organizations. Why do conflicts escalate? And how can they be resolved? Dame Rennie Fritchie DBE and Malcolm Leary outline the nature of group conflicts in organizations and provide strategies to resolve them,offering you:

- a framework to recognise the characteristics of particular conflict and how individual temperaments react to different kinds of conflict
- an understanding of how conflicts in groups can escalate
- the skills needed to resolve conflict at different levels of escalation.

"Not only very interesting but also I'm sure that many organizations will find it extremely useful."

Philip Holton,
Head of Management & Organization Development, NHS Executive.

"Extremely informative and of great practical use. The interactive exercises* included in the book are a particularly Interesting innovation, they involve me in the subject matter and help me formulate a plan of action."

Fiona Halstead, Exeter Community NHS Trust.

About the Authors

Dame Rennie Fritchie's career has spanned many fields including major chairing roles in the National Health Service. She is the co-author of *The Business of Assertiveness*. **Malcolm Leary** is a consultant and researcher with many clients in the UK and throughout the world. He is the co-founder of Transform and a partner, along with Dame Rennie Fritchie, of The Conflict Challenge.

ISBN 1-898001-45-6